TEACHER
SELF-EVALUATION

TEACHER
SELF-EVALUATION

Ray H. Simpson

PROFESSOR OF EDUCATIONAL
PSYCHOLOGY
UNIVERSITY OF ILLINOIS

THE MACMILLAN COMPANY, NEW YORK
COLLIER-MACMILLAN LIMITED, LONDON

Second Printing, 1966

Library of Congress catalog card number: 66-14214

THE MACMILLAN COMPANY, NEW YORK
COLLIER-MACMILLAN CANADA, LTD., TORONTO, ONTARIO

Printed in the United States of America

Preface

BEFORE THE NOVICE embarks on a career of teaching, excellent preparation is obviously important. Equally if not more important is continuous systematic professional growth on the part of the instructor during his active teaching career. The "knowledge explosion," the changing needs of those taught, and the increased research in psychology and sociology should all give increasing emphasis to growth on the job. Systematic professional growth can very appropriately set an example of meaningful and useful learning for pupils. This type of growth, which is wholeheartedly endorsed by teacher organizations, can combat the serious teacher dropout problem by encouraging more satisfying and productive experiences for teachers. These ideas are explored in Chapter 1.

Self-evaluation procedures are, or should be, of concern to prospective teachers and new teachers, as well as to experienced teachers. Chapter 2 suggests some procedures and tools with which the instructor should be familiar if he is systematically to implement his self-diagnosis and self-improvement.

Self-evaluation ideally should be initiated by the student who is in training for teaching. Preceding and during student teaching, as well as in the crucial period of position selection, the preprofessional should be prepared to assess his or her strengths and weaknesses. In Chapter 3 are suggested areas for self-evaluation important to the novice and to the experienced teacher who may be considering a change of position.

In a world of rapidly expanding knowledge in practically every subject matter field, it is incumbent upon the teacher that he systematically and regularly expand his horizons of knowledge. Some ways of diagnosing current knowledge and of enlarging perspective are explored in Chapter 4.

The effectiveness of the learning of the individual pupil is directly correlated with the extent to which the implicit classroom goals and procedures are appropriate for him. Issues are raised in Chapter 5 which are designed to help the teacher decide where and how he can improve his goal-setting and classroom procedures. Almost all American teachers attempt to use textbooks as the basic organizers of pupil learning. For this reason the alert teacher is constantly searching for ways to improve the selection and use of these organizers for learning. Chapter 6 suggests approaches the instructor may use to make textbook selection and utilization more effective processes.

Although difficult to assess precisely, there is no doubt that a teacher's personality has an important bearing on his pupil's learning. Chapter 7 is designed to help the teacher diagnose and improve such aspects of personality as his self-perception, his perceptions of others, and his behavior which reflects his professional personality.

The modern teacher does not operate in isolation; he works reciprocally with other professionals, giving as well as receiving help. Working with other professionals not only involves text selection and curriculum construction, but also, through exchanging new ideas on crucial educational issues and accepting and offering constructive criticism, helps teachers keep professionally alive. Chapter 8 sets forth some of the ways in which colleagues interact with teachers.

Significant improvements in educational practice can come only through systematic improvement in the individual teacher. We hope this book will help teachers toward this improvement.

R. H. S.

Contents

TEACHER
SELF-EVALUATION

1

Why Is Teacher Self-evaluation Needed?

Excellent teacher preparation and superior teaching demand continuous attention to problems of teacher self-evaluation and its avowed goal—teacher self-improvement. Mere teaching experience will not guarantee improvement. In fact, the teacher who does not achieve professional growth and improved teaching behaviors is bound to slide back. That the problem of achieving professional growth is a serious one is pointed out in a study by Swineford[1] of factors that affect teaching behavior. He concluded that a "comparison of student and field teacher ratings points up the fallacy of assuming higher competence with years of field experience. Half the teachers studied were still teaching very much as they were in student teaching."[2] Improvement in teaching does not come automatically, and the teacher who continues year after year to rely almost exclusively on what he learned in his undergraduate teacher training is bound to fall farther and farther behind from a professional standpoint. Self-evaluation can form the basis for rational change and can help the instructor to systematically allocate a reasonable amount of time and effort for self-improvement in the areas where he believes changes are likely to be most profitable.

Three pronounced challenges impinge strongly and with increasing urgency on the modern teacher. These three challenges

[1] E. J. Swineford, "A Study of Factors that Affect Teaching Behavior," *California Journal of Educational Research*, **14** (November 1963), pp. 214–224.

[2] *Ibid.*, p. 224.

are directly related to the "knowledge explosion," to the changing needs of those taught, and to the increased research in psychology, sociology, and related fields which is relevant to teaching and learning.

The "knowledge explosion" represents a primary challenge to the alert teacher. In many subject matter fields, knowledge is expanding at a phenomenal rate. Experts tell us that in some fields knowledge is doubling every ten years. To keep even reasonably up to date in the subject matter fields in which he teaches, the instructor must systematically grow.

A second major challenge revolves around the changing educational needs that characterize those taught. Not only is more education demanded in the modern world but also different kinds of education are needed if the real challenge is to be met. Two related factors may be mentioned for illustrative purposes. The rapid expansion of automation increasingly demands skills and abilities some of which were not even dreamed of twenty years ago. The serious nature of the problem is illustrated in New York City where there are 54,000 white collar jobs unfilled for lack of qualified applicants, while 77,000 unemployed out-of-school youths are unable to find work.[3] Also, an educational system which has been tooled largely to prepare for work activities must concern itself with provisions for vastly increased leisure time. Reports indicating 700,000 annual loss[4] in "school dropouts" suggest the magnitude of the problem implicit in this second big challenge, changing educational needs to those taught.

A third major challenge to the teacher is presented in the rapidly increasing amount of educational research which can help the teacher to do a better job if he will but become acquainted with it. Illustrative of the voluminous research of recent years are the *Handbook of Research on Teaching*[5] (1,218 double-columned pages) and the *Encyclopedia of Educational Research*[6] (1,520) large, double-columned pages). Research results

[3] R. D. Strom, *The Tragic Migration* (Washington, D.C.: National Education Association, 1964).

[4] *Ibid.*

[5] N. L. Gage, *Handbook of Research on Teaching* (Chicago: Rand, McNally and Co., 1963).

[6] C. W. Harris (ed.), *Encyclopedia of Educational Research*, 3rd ed. (New York: The Macmillan Company, 1960).

are continually being produced on such subjects as the merits of programmed learning, the values of team teaching, the ungraded vs. the graded plans of organization, and a host of other issues which merit the continued concern of the teacher who wishes to keep professionally alive.

Some of the new challenges faced by the teacher have been indicated by Kinney.[7]

Changes in education come more slowly than we might wish, and as we adjust to them we take them for granted. Yet Rip [Van Winkle], as a [twentieth-century] teacher, might be puzzled by the emphasis on meaning in arithmetic which he would find in the modern textbook in contrast with the emphasis on rote memory in the "thirties." He would need to adapt his thinking to another swing of the curricular pendulum, since the high schools are now preparing over half their graduates for college entrance, while a quarter of a century ago only around ten per cent were headed for college. His practices would need to be reoriented to new social needs, as he learns that during his sleep we went through a depression, World War II, and are now embarked on a "cold" war with shortages in crucial areas of trained leadership.

. . . During his professional lifetime he [the teacher] is expected practically to re-educate himself. . . . The continued growth of the teacher in professional competence whether by individual effort, by organized in-service programs, or by advanced work in preparing institutions, is accordingly a social necessity. The programs of teacher preparation reflect to some extent this necessity for self-directed growth. The teacher not only learns the methodology of his profession, but also its scientific and social foundations. Self-directed growth depends also on frequent self-evaluation of his own effectiveness, in the light of a clearly defined criterion of professional competence, on the basis of adequate evidence. Such self-evaluation is useful only for the teacher who has defined and accepted an adequate criterion, can collect evidence on his own effectiveness, and can direct his own education.

At this point it might be well to describe the contrasting approaches of two teachers faced with similar problems. In December a few years back a fifth-grade teacher, Miss Winters, and her principal called in the parents of Steve and told them Steve would have to be taken out of the school. The list of offenses against him was long, including being a troublemaker,

<hr />

[7] L. B. Kinney, "Self-evaluation: The Mark of a Profession," *Educational Leadership*, 15 (1958), pp. 228–231. Copyright © 1958 by the Association for Supervision and Curriculum Development. Reprinted by permission.

being unwilling to follow directions of the teacher, being unwilling to do the assignments made by the teacher, pestering other students in the class, and a host of other weaknesses.

No mention was made by Miss Winters or her principal of possible weaknesses on *their* part which were, no doubt, key factors in the eventual expulsion of Steve from the school. To understand Steve's problem better we may go back to the preceding August when the list of books each parent was supposed to buy for his fifth grader was published in the local papers. Steve's connection with one of these books, a fifth-grade speller, can give us some insight into the teaching-learning situation of which he was a part. On the first day of school Steve told his teacher that he thought he could spell all of the words in the spelling book. Miss Winters pronounced five or six of the more difficult words near the back of the book, and sure enough Steve spelled them all correctly. The subsequent pattern for spelling in Miss Winters' classroom was as follows: Monday: Assignment of 25 words from speller with each word to be written 25 times by Tuesday and 25 more times by Wednesday. Wednesday: "Pretest" on words assigned on Monday. And words missed on the pretest were to be written 25 times each by Thursday and 25 times again by Friday. On Friday a retest was given to all students over all the words whether missed or not. On each subsequent week the same basic pattern was followed without deviation.

How did Steve and other pupils react to this routine and unimaginative spelling program? As might be expected, discipline was a serious problem, and Miss Winters had to spend much of her time "keeping order." After two weeks Steve reminded his teacher that he already knew how to spell the words and saw no sense in writing each word 25 times on Monday and again on Tuesday. Miss Winters' only reaction was that perhaps he needed writing practice. Incidentally, test records from the preceding spring showed that Steve had a spelling achievement level of 8.8, approximately three grade levels above the average fifth grader. After three or four weeks of school Steve simply refused to write the spelling words 25 times each, since he already knew how to spell them. There were other pupils in the class who regularly missed 23 or more words on the pretest and approximately the same number on the retest. Their assignment was identical to Steve's.

In comments to each other, it was clear that the teacher and the principal were definitely working on the assumption that all the fault lay with Steve and other class members and none with a school system that encouraged the use of inappropriate materials for the individual child and none with a teacher who gave totally inappropriate assignments and who was not even attempting to diagnose some of her own weaknesses.

Contrast the behavior of Miss Winters with that of another fifth-grade teacher, Miss Sharp, who taught in a community similar to that of Miss Winters. In the year preceding the one with which we are concerned, Miss Sharp's teaching approaches were similar to those of Miss Winters, and she was plagued with similar problems. However, Miss Sharp, partially as a result of some in-service training in an extramural class, decided to do something constructive about the situation by diagnosing her own leadership characteristics and by planning to improve them.

A pretest was still given, but on Monday, not on Wednesday. Students thereafter needed to pay no more attention to words they knew how to spell. Advanced students took turns in dictating words to their peers after preparing an appropriate sentence to illustrate each word. While this was being done, Miss Sharp had time to devote to other activities. Also, students got some practice in a nontension-producing leadership role which prepared some, particularly those who were shy, to later give talks before the class.

Professional reading and observation of other teachers led Miss Sharp to try out many approaches. A sympathetic principal and an extramural instructor encouraged observations and also encouraged the teacher to study and improve. One of the most successful approaches Miss Sharp found in her study was that of having each child make up his own list of spelling words each week. The list was based on the words he had missed in *his* writing in other subjects in the preceding week which had been identified by either himself, a peer, or Miss Sharp. These individually custom-tailored lists were in the writing vocabulary of the child—hence, were particularly important for his spelling. More peer leadership was developed by having youngsters pair off and "test" each other by pronouncing each other's words at the end of the week.

While the "text" was still used to a degree, Miss Sharp found more and more time was devoted to words the pupils themselves helped to identify as ones they needed to learn to spell. "Spelling demon" lists of words were brought to class and used, particularly by advanced students. Charts were kept by the individual child of the number of words he had learned how to spell.

Space does not permit more details of the new Miss Sharp's classroom. However, the contrast between Miss Winter's and Miss Sharp's classrooms gradually became striking after the latter decided she, the major classroom leader, was primarily responsible for improvement of the teaching-learning situation therein. The following year Miss Sharp became a member of the school text committee and was instrumental in helping the school move from a single-text system to a multitext arrangement to better provide the kinds of materials needed to take care of individual differences in the school.

It is recognized that most readers may not be spelling teachers. However, the same basic psychological problems faced by Miss Winter and by Miss Sharp are constantly being faced by all teachers regardless of the particular subject taught. The basic question is: Will we take the Winter's approach and blame lack of satisfactory learning on the pupils, or will we adopt the Sharp assumption that the teacher can and should diagnose *his* weaknesses and constantly work on correcting them?

SELF-EVALUATION CAN HELP THE TEACHER TO DEFINE HIS ROLE

If the teacher is to become a true professional he must clarify his primary role. Superficially this might seem to be simple enough. However, it has been estimated that about one-third of the teacher's day goes to clerical and subprofessional tasks.[8] Trump suggests that another third goes to work which could just as well be done by automated devices. If these estimates

[8] J. L. Trump and D. Baynham, *Focus on Change* (Chicago: Rand, McNally and Co., 1961).

are approximately correct, then only a third of a day goes for performance of work the teacher is primarily trained to do and in which the teacher finds satisfaction doing. As Boy and Pine[9] have pointed out, "If a teacher does not define his role, if he does not develop a professional identity, then someone else will describe his function for him." They further point out one way in which teachers' roles *might be* defined by *teachers* by suggesting the following as proper functions for the teacher:

1. Engage in quality teaching, i.e., teaching which reflects depth of knowledge and which is based upon the empirical evidence of research. . . .
2. Function as a curriculum specialist in his specific subject or at his particular grade level. . . .
3. Conduct research designed to measure the effectiveness of his teaching and to improve instructional materials and methods. The professional teacher will also be aware of and make use of the research findings applicable to his subjects and level of instruction.
4. Motivate students to learn by using imaginative and creative teaching and learning approaches, and by developing instruction and curriculum which is meaningful to the student and which meets his needs.
5. Keep abreast of current developments and new knowledge in his subject field and his chosen profession of education.
6. Prepare instruction and up-to-date teaching and tools.
7. Function as a resource consultant to other professional personnel in providing services to meet the needs of each individual student.

Tasks too frequently handled by teachers but which Boy and Pine feel should be handled either by other professionals or by clerical aids, volunteers from PTA's, faculty secretaries, teacher aids, and other subprofessionals include:

1. Clerical tasks which prevent him from devoting his full effort to professional work. For example: collecting fees, mimeographing tests and class exercises; ordering supplies; keeping grade books, class records, and health records; scoring tests; soliciting subscriptions to magazines; distributing, collecting, and alphabetizing various forms; recording test data; or arranging bus transportation for field trips.

[9] A. V. Boy and G. J. Pine, "Needed for Teachers: A Role Description," *The Clearing House*, 38 (September 1963), pp. 7–12. The excerpts that follow are reprinted by permission.

2. Performing supervisory duties such as hall patrol, cafeteria supervision, study hall supervision, bus supervision, or supervision of detention halls.
3. Potpourri functions—the teacher is not a psychologist, a psychometrician, a counselor, a social worker, a physician, a nurse, a truant officer, or a baby sitter.
4. Public relations work for various community agencies and organizations which interferes with the teaching function within the classroom.

The teacher may need to diagnose the roles teacher organizations to which he belongs are or should be taking to help clarify professional roles.

Boy and Pine[10] concluded: "Unless the sleeping giant awakens, unless teachers become involved in defining and redefining their role, there is the strong possibility that the small percentage of time currently available for teaching will be even more greatly diminished as time passes. The ultimate loss will be to the students who pass through our schools." Reassessment of teacher roles and functional implementation of sound professional roles will demand cooperation among teachers and administrators.

Self-evaluation Can Help Combat Teacher Dropouts

Much has been written in recent years about dropout problems with students. This concern with learner dropouts is certainly justified; however, the shocking annual dropout rate among teachers has been given insufficient attention. Careful estimates indicate that the schools lose over 10 per cent of their teachers each year through turnover. This means that the teaching profession is losing over 135,000 classroom teachers each year through dropouts.[11]

A study by Nelson and Thompson[12] indicates that only 75 per

[10] *Ibid.,* p. 12.

[11] W. S. Mason and R. K. Bain, *Teacher Turnover in the Public Schools, 1957–1958* (Washington, D.C.: Government Printing Office, 1959), U.S. Office of Education Circular No. 608.

[12] R. H. Nelson and M. L. Thompson, "Why Teachers Quit," *The Clearing House,* 37 (1963), p. 467.

cent of people prepared to teach actually enter the classroom. "Worse yet, however, fewer than ten per cent of this three-fourths will be found in the classroom ten years hence." This, in effect, means that of every 1,000 teachers trained, only 750 actually enter the classroom. Of the 750, less than 75 will be in the classroom ten years after training ended. Thus, we start by training 1,000 teachers and end up with 75 ten years later, a terrible professional mortality.

There are, of course, many reasons why teachers quit, but no doubt one of the most important of these is lack of continuing satisfaction with experiences in the classroom. For example, a nationwide survey of teacher turnover reports "that higher-paying suburban school districts have as much turnover as rural areas where salaries are traditionally lower." The researchers go on to say that "dissatisfaction with the school system, not low salaries, was first among causes of turnover. Salary alone does not hold teachers."[13] A sound and constructive way through which to combat teacher "dropoutitis" is the development of systematic self-evaluation which can make teaching a challenging and exhilarating experience rather than a deadening and boring routine.

Self-evaluation can help the teacher avoid the boring rut that finally becomes so stifling that he feels he must escape it entirely. This over 90 per cent apparently do over a ten-year period.

EXAMPLE IS STRONGER THAN PRECEPT

The teacher's stock in trade is, of course, the encouragement of learning. Verbal telling of others to learn is not enough; a personal example of systematic learning is desperately needed if the pupils are to take very seriously what the teacher says about the desirability of such activity. For example, the teacher whose assignments and other class procedures provoke disciplinary problems and who continues to make the same kinds of assignments and uses the same class routines is not likely to be highly regarded by his students. On the other hand, the teacher is more likely to be respected by students if he evaluates the

[13] *Educational Digest,* **29** (March 1964), p. 57.

probable causes of difficulties in the teaching-learning situation, studies possible improvement steps, and then follows through with revised activities designed to correct some of the difficulties. Pupils are likely to recognize that this teacher believes in learning and behavior adaptation enough to utilize them himself.

Consider the teacher who is trying to train pupils to read and use ideas in English, science, or social science. He is likely to have much greater effectiveness if it is clear to the pupils that he himself is using professional reading material to improve himself in his chosen profession. The example a teacher sets by continuously and systematically learning himself can convince learners that the teacher believes enough in the type of thing he is encouraging them to do to actually do it himself.

Professional Groups Favor Teacher Self-evaluation

It is important to clearly differentiate between teacher evaluation for salary adjustment purposes and teacher self-evaluation designed to help the teacher improve professionally. Most teacher groups have consistently opposed "merit" rating for salary determination. For example, a Study Conference on Merit Rating sponsored by the Department of Classroom Teachers[14] "registered their unqualified opposition to merit rating as a basis for salary scheduling. . . . To substantiate their opposition to merit rating, the conferees cited many ways in which they believed merit rating hurts the profession, conflicts with good teaching techniques, has harmful effects on the pupil, hinders good teacher-administrator relationships, hampers the community, and impedes the adjustment to teachers salaries."

Regardless of the accuracy of the sentiments expressed in the preceding paragraph, few teachers or professional groups seem to have any opposition to teacher self-evaluation. In fact, most professional teacher groups are enthusiastic about teacher self-evaluation, recognizing its crucial role in promoting self-improvement. The study group referred to in the preceding

[14] *Classroom Teachers Speak on Merit Rating* (Washington, D.C.: National Education Association, 1957), p. 5.

paragraph emphasized this: "The classroom teacher should strive for constant self-examination and group evaluation."[15]

The significant role that national teachers' professional associations believe evaluation should play in professional growth is well summarized by a pamphlet prepared by the Commission on Teacher Evaluation of the Association for Supervision and Curriculum Development:[16]

Evaluation is part of the process by which people make choices and come to decisions. Through this process, individuals or groups make choices which affect the direction of their growth. The purpose of education is to assist people toward better living by helping them improve the quality of their choices. As a result of their school living, people should be enabled to arrive at more intelligent decisions than would be possible for them without these experiences.

Teacher self-evaluation is almost unanimously recommended by teacher organizations and professional experts on teacher improvement. Regardless of the extent of disagreement on other characteristics of good teachers there is almost universal consensus that self-improvement based on self-evaluation is both desirable and crucial. Some important improvements in education may demand significant institutional changes. However, there are a multitude of points at which the individual teacher can improve without significant institutional changes.

[15] *Ibid.*, p. 12.
[16] *Better Than Rating* (Washington, D.C.: National Education Association, 1950).

2

Self-evaluation:
Procedures and Tools

THE INSTRUCTOR who wants to go about the important task of improving his effectiveness almost always can get help from the great variety of tools and procedures that have been found useful by other teachers. Typically, it is desirable for the teacher periodically to conduct some type or types of self-diagnosis. Such diagnosis will likely show he is relatively strong in some areas of his professional activities. The diagnosis will also point out to the teacher some areas in which he is relatively weak and in which improvement is to be desired. For example, one teacher using Cosgrove's, "The Descriptive Ranking Form for Teachers,"[1] found she was particularly strong in (1) knowledge and organization of subject matter, and (2) adequacy of plans and procedures in class. She also found that she was relatively weak in (1) adequacy of relations with students in class, and (2) enthusiasm in working with students. One reasonable approach for this teacher is to do some careful and intensive study of some of the wealth of research studies in the general field of social psychology, including such subdivisions as leadership, development of peer- and self-leadership in classes, improving class climate, and use of groups and grouping. Such studies can result in improved interpersonal relations in the classroom.

In order to diagnose effectively it is very desirable that the teacher become acquainted with the great arsenal of tools and

[1] D. J. Cosgrove, "Diagnostic Rating of Teacher Performance," *Journal of Educational Psychology,* **50** (1959), pp. 200–204.

procedures available to him. The following paragraphs contain a picture of some of the types of tools and procedures that the teacher should at least be cognizant of so that he can select those which he believes are likely to be most helpful to him.

INSTRUCTOR'S WRITTEN ASSESSMENT OF HIS TEACHING

To set the stage for systematic change in activities that will result in improvement, it is desirable for the instructor continually to diagnose what he is doing, why he is doing it, and how it is succeeding.

One of the ways of collecting data that will encourage self-improvement involves framing and answering questions that will help the teacher view objectively his current inadequacies and so help him chart the directions in which he wants to grow professionally. Teachers, inveterate testers of their pupils, are invited by Simpson[2] to apply the testing processes to some of their own activities. For self-diagnostic purposes, the individual teacher is encouraged to evaluate himself on 33 questions. Questions relate to three main areas, and illustrative examples follow:

1. Provision for individual differences in academic ability.
   Examples: In the last year did I have as much concern for the very rapid learner as for the very slow learner? Did I help provide reading materials for daily use which had a spread in difficulty of at least five grades.
2. Provision for professional development.
   Examples: During the last year, did I participate *actively* in teachers' meetings? Did I read at least four professional magazines in the average month?
3. Provision for aiding youngsters in developing socially.
   Examples: During the last year, did I encourage pupils to study and work out many of their problems together? Did I discuss more than once with pupils the problem of how to work more effectively with others in a committee?

Another type of instructor self-evaluation involves writing down after each class period what the instructor himself feels

[2] R. H. Simpson, "Teachers, Here Is Your Final," *The Clearing House,* **16** (September 1941), pp. 47–48.

were the strong points and weak points during the teaching-learning situation under consideration. While such an evaluation may take three to seven minutes of instructor time, it can be quite helpful, if it is done periodically, in showing the teacher places where he believes additional attention is needed in his instruction.

A third type of written assessment which many teachers have found helpful is one made at the end of each semester or each year. Such an assessment can include types of things the teacher feels went successfully during the year as well as areas where the teacher thinks improvement would be very desirable. Such lists, if done carefully, can provide the teacher with a basis for changing materials that are used, changing assignments, modifying class procedures, and other types of things which have been identified by the teacher as needing modifications.

STUDENT ACHIEVEMENT

The acid test of teaching, of course, revolves around the achievements of learners. This suggests that it is important for the teacher to attempt systematic follow-up of former students, both those in school and those out of school, in order to get suggestions for improvement.

Some primary teachers have found it helpful to talk with pupils they have had who have moved into the intermediate level, and question them as to what difficulties they are currently having. In a similar fashion, intermediate teachers have interviewed high school students. And additionally, high school teachers have found it helpful to follow up, either on vacations or by means of correspondence, students who have gone to college or who have gone into jobs in the community. Some instructors have found it desirable to help *current* students interview a certain number of the teacher's past students. This not only can provide useful feedback to the teacher but sometimes improves current motivation among students and helps them to understand better the purposes and possible future uses of a course.

Another way of checking on student achievement is to list teaching objectives and then to use structured tests, either teacher-made or commercial, to see the extent to which objectives are being achieved. An important feature of this activity is to first list objectives specifically and then attempt to find tests that seem to measure these objectives. Oral testing of students' achievement should not be neglected. Interviewing a sampling of students may improve the teacher's perspective.

Some teachers have found it stimulating to make a comparative check of their own efficiency using one technique or approach as compared with efficiency in using another, different technique or approach either with different groups or in two semesters. For example, one junior high school teacher, concerned over poor mathematical growth in her students the preceding year, decided to make some changes and to measure the results. She recalled that when she had been an elementary teacher of reading she had learned to make adjustments to individual students' abilities in learning to read. She had used two, three, or four groups of pupils reading from different books and using different materials. She decided to try something similar in her junior high school mathematics classes in the following year.

In brief her plan, evolved largely the preceding summer, was characterized by the following: use of a pretest on the first day of classes to determine individual abilities in mathematics; use of three different texts, acquired with the help of her principal; varied assignments, the one for a particular child depending upon his stage of mathematical development; development of much self-responsibility in self-assignment making on the part of individual pupils; use of peer help and leadership; and finally a retest at the end of each semester. The results of retest were compared with pretest scores to obtain an indication of mathematical growth. When growth with the revised setup was compared with that of the preceding year, the teacher was very pleased, particularly with significantly greater gains in word and thought problems.

Work with Colleagues

The process whereby a teacher committee gets together in a workshop to discuss or to construct a teacher-evaluation instrument or questionnaire can be a very stimulating activity, particularly for those who are directly involved in the workshop or in the committee. Regardless of what subsequent use is made of the questionnaire or evaluation instrument that is discussed or produced, the actual process of developing it is in itself an excellent type of in-service activity.

Team teaching is a much emphasized arrangement in recent years which offers great possibilities for teacher self-evaluation. Team teaching is, of course, a way of organizing the instructional program and may be used on either the elementary or the secondary level. Cooperating teaching groups may work vertically (that is, at all grade levels in a single subject or similar subjects); or they may work horizontally (that is, at one grade level but in several subjects). In any case, members of a team set up objectives together, plan together to achieve these objectives, talk freely with each other, and are constantly assisting and assessing each other. It is this latter feature which offers great promise in helping the teacher in self-diagnosis. As each teacher works with other members of his team he can gain stimulation through comparing his strengths and weaknesses with those of others on his team. The spirit of frankness that is characteristic of a well-functioning team permits the teacher to get direct and indirect reactions of colleagues to various aspects of his teaching.

Regularly planned meetings of all of those teaching at a certain grade level or in a particular course permit the teacher to obtain the suggestions of colleagues relative to his objectives, plans, and procedures. Such regular meetings or seminars should meet on school time, and a frank discussion of points of view relative to proposals is essential. One plan of operation involves having one teacher responsible at each meeting for presenting to colleagues something he is doing or is planning or has read about in a professional journal. A free exchange of ideas permits the teacher to make some evaluation of his ideas and procedures through the continuous verbal interchanges with colleagues. The exchanging of staff ideas is frequently facilitated by regular small group luncheons where the avowed purpose of the discussion is to evaluate the teaching proposals and practices of those involved.

In many schools such specialists as the administrator, the supervisor, or the guidance specialist have the time, knowhow, and willingness to help the teacher in his self-assessment. For this to happen in a beneficial way it is usually necessary for the teacher to request such help. When this is done, it is frequently taken as a sign of strength on the part of the teacher that he is willing to request aid in self-diagnosis. Such aid may involve conferences with the teacher, observations in the teacher's classroom, getting feedback from students, or other information about some aspects of the teaching-learning situation about which the teacher is concerned. The guidance specialist may, for example, help the teacher diagnose the social-emotional climate for learning in the teacher's classroom by suggesting tests, inventories, or other approaches. For best results, (1) the teacher should request the help, (2) the interaction between teacher and specialist should go on over a considerable period of time, and (3) the teacher should give ideas and insights a tryout which then should be followed by an assessment of effectiveness.

An exchange program of materials and observations can be mutually stimulating to the instructors concerned. In such a program, two or more instructors agree to supply the other cooperating person involved with the professional materials, diagnostic tests, and other materials that have been found particularly useful. Also, a reciprocal type of class observation is set up in which each teacher observes the other teaching and then offers suggestions on how the situation might be improved. Many administrators are willing to provide teacher substitutes or other arrangements to make such a plan for diagnosis and improvement possible.

For greatest value from shared materials and observation, those involved must desire this type of stimulating interaction; frankness and reciprocated confidence must be shown; and sufficient time must be provided not only for the observations but also for the conferences which should typically be held subsequent to each activity.

The possibility of setting up such reciprocal aid in diagnosis with teachers in other parts of the school system or even with teachers in neighboring systems should not be neglected. A local organization of classroom teachers can sometimes appropriately take the lead in sponsoring reciprocal observations and in getting necessary administrative arrangements made for them.

Professional Reading and Self-evaluation

The well-trained teacher increasingly appreciates the wealth of help that professional reading can provide. A key area of help involves the discovery, analysis, and use of tools for self-evaluation. Descriptions and discussions of such tools regularly appear in such periodicals as *The School Review, Harvard Educational Review, The Clearing House, The Journal of Educational Psychology, Educational Leadership,* and the *Phi Delta Kappan.* The new experimental studies involving teacher-evaluation tools with potential implications for the teacher must be continuously assayed.

The tests and inventories for investigating teacher reading skills and practices, for example, have provided some interesting and thought-provoking conclusions. Much has been written about reading disabilities, but educators sometimes forget that they themselves may suffer from such liabilities. For example, in a large urban school system it was found that 3 per cent of the twelfth-grade pupils actually read better than 100 per cent of the teachers.[3] The educators were found to be particularly low on these subtests of the Iowa Silent Reading Test: selection of key words, use of index, and directed reading.

The diagnosis further revealed that a reasonable amount of leisure-time, recreational reading was done by the teachers, but little or no professional reading to help solve school problems was engaged in by the typical teacher or administrator. Unfortunately, even those teachers who scored high on the reading test, which indicated that they knew how to read well, made little if any more professional use of this ability than did those who scored low. A study of 746 teachers and administrators indicated the following results related to professional reading for a particular month:

No magazine articles read 14%
One magazine article read 10%
Two magazine articles read 13%
Three to five magazine articles read 29%

[3] R. H. Simpson, "Reading Disabilities Among Teachers and Administrators," *The Clearing House,* 17 (1942), p. 12.

More than five magazine articles read 34%
Had not even looked at one professional book 40%
Had sampled one book 17%
Had read parts of two books 24%
Had read parts of three to five books 15%
Had read parts of five or more books 4%

When the results of this type of diagnosis face the individual teacher or the group, it is likely that some decisions will be made to change the situation.

ANALYSIS OF CLASS SESSIONS

One way to set the stage for systematic change in activities that will result in improvement is to make tape recordings or even television recordings of regular class sessions and then make a feedback analysis. Modern recording devices that are relatively inexpensive permit a fairly accurate pickup in classroom situations. This permits the teacher to analyze such things as the following: What he said and how much of the time he was talking, what the students said, how many students participated, the kinds of questions students raised, if any. Also such mechanical features as the quality of the teacher's voice and the speech of students can be helpfully studied under some circumstances. Some teachers have been amazed at the sounds of their own voices in the classroom. Where a teacher has not used this approach it can be very stimulating.

Another related type of tape recording can be made of an evaluative class session in which strengths and limitations of the class are analyzed by the students. This type of recording is usually made during the middle of a semester or year so that the teacher can use the leads that are picked up in improving his instruction. Such a discussion may be led by the instructor himself, or by a student, or by a panel of students, or in some cases by a colleague who has been invited into the class for this particular purpose and who is known to be able to quickly establish desirable rapport with students. Such an atmosphere is necessary for an evaluative class session to be a frank revealing of how students feel about various class activities.

USE OF THE WHOLE CLASS FOR GETTING SELF-EVALUATION LEADS

A variety of techniques are available for use with the whole class in alerting the teacher as to what his students consider to be relatively strong and weak aspects of his performance. Such evaluation can be useful to the instructor who desires to know where to begin to work on improving his effectiveness.

Postclass reaction sheets, filled out in the last two or three minutes of a particular class period or at the end of the morning or afternoon, with appropriately selected questions can give the teacher some indication of students' reactions to what is happening to them in the classroom. Such questions as the following can elicit useful leads: What did you like about today's class period? What part of today's class period do you think should be changed, if any? In today's class period did the teacher give sufficient opportunity for discussion? Did the teacher clarify issues? Was too much time used by a few students. Did the teacher encourage all to participate in discussions? Did the teacher maintain a good balance between pupil and teacher participation? If such questions are asked at appropriately spaced intervals during the semester or year, the teacher at least can see how students are reacting to some class activities.

Another whole class activity is to encourage students to elect a committee that will develop a learning-evaluation questionnaire to be answered by the whole class. The construction of such a questionnaire in and of itself can be useful in developing a consciousness on the part of class members of the purposes involved in the learning and also tends to help develop student responsibility. The school may itself want to encourage the student council or some representative student group to construct a learning-evaluation instrument. In all cases, teacher guidance should be given in the consideration of goals to be checked and in the development of the instrument. Also, a battery of suggestive evaluative items such as those in *Student Evaluation of Teaching and Learning*[4] can suggest to students and teacher what to include in a questionnaire.

[4] R. H. Simpson and J. M. Seidman, *Student Evaluation of Teaching and Learning* (Washington, D.C.: The American Association of Colleges for Teacher Education, 1962).

Another stimulating way to get ideas for self-improvement is to have one class period, or a part of such, periodically devoted to course planning. This may involve planning for the present class or may take place near the end of the year to give the teacher suggestions for the following year. Such planning sessions can give the teacher some idea of student-perceived strengths and weaknesses of the current class. Such topic areas as the following can provide a basis for discussion: To what extent have the goals and purposes of this class been clear? What are reactions to the text materials we have been using? How have you reacted as students to the assignments that have been made? Have they given you sufficient opportunity to make choices and decisions so that you would not be doing busy work? Have you seen the importance of the types of activities you have been asked to do in this class? Has the amount of time you feel you have been expected to spend on the class been reasonably appropriate?

Some teachers have found that asking students to write answers to such questions as the following is useful: What do you regard as this class's major strengths? What possible weaknesses do you see in the work of the class to date? How could these weaknesses be diminished? What do you consider to be the one or more best features of this course? What are the one or more least satisfactory features of the course? What suggestions do you have for improving this course?

The growing body of research literature on the use of students' rating of their teachers indicates that pupils can and do make reasonably accurate ratings of teachers. As Howsam[5] reports:

Their ratings tend to agree with each other, and the teachers who are rated best by the pupils tend to obtain the highest pupil gains. Pupil ratings often do not agree with ratings by principals, supervisors, or other teachers. (This has not been considered an indication of weakness [of student ratings], however, since ratings by superiors and peers have not been shown to agree with pupil-gained measures or to be satisfactory in other ways.) Teachers have indicated their belief that pupil ratings, as obtained in research studies, are both fair and accurate.

[5] R. B. Howsam, *Who's a Good Teacher?* (1705 Merchanson Drive, Burlingame, California: Joint Committee on Personnel Procedures, 1960).

These research findings would seem to indicate that teachers should consider making more use of evaluative questionnaires, checklists, or inventories which either are self-constructed or have been borrowed from such sources as *Student Evaluation of Teaching and Learning.*[6]

USE OF SELECTED INDIVIDUAL PUPILS

There are several techniques involving individual learners that some teachers have found helpful. One of these is to have a nonclass member who is an accelerated pupil periodically observe and evaluate selected class sessions. When this is done, it is usually necessary for the teacher to alert the observer to the dimensions on which he is to consider the class. Sometimes an observation sheet developed by the teacher will greatly facilitate the recording of the observer's reactions.

Another procedure is to have regular or periodic informal discussions with individual pupils. Consideration should be given to getting reactions from various levels of intellectual ability. For example, the reactions and opinions of some average pupil should be sampled. Also the teacher may wish to elicit the judgments of bright or "reliable" learners who seem to be quite perceptive and who are able and willing to talk about various aspects of the class. A third group of individuals that the teacher may want to make use of in this regard are poor or relatively weak pupils who may have quite a different perception of such things as assignments, class discussions, text materials, and work expected by the teacher.

Another technique is to have a different pupil each day assume the role of class evaluator. This learner would, at the beginning of the period, be provided with an evaluation sheet by the teacher. This sheet would indicate types of things at which the class evaluator is suppose to look. One advantage of this approach, aside from the aid it may give to the teacher in self-evaluation, is that it may help learners become more involved in the planning, leadership, and responsibility for the class, and consequently it may favorably affect motivation.

In addition to "keeping his ear to the ground" for various

---

[6] Simpson and Seidman, *op. cit.*

evidences of student reaction to classroom activities, the teacher may wish to have elected by the students an evaluation committee which will meet with him periodically and provide feedback to him on student reactions to various activities, assignments, marking procedures, testing procedures, and other important aspects of the class.

In conclusion, it may be pointed out that evaluation of teaching-learning situations is continuously being made by teachers, students, administrators, parents, and others. Whether this evaluation will be soundly grounded depends to a high degree on the type of evidence upon which it is based. If the teacher wishes to improve his base for evaluation, one of the best ways is to develop a familiarity with, and a use of, a variety of measurement tools. A few of these have been suggested in the preceding paragraphs.

3

Self-evaluation and a New Position

THERE ARE a number of questions that the teacher or the prospective teacher needs to raise with himself in looking forward to a new position. These are concerned primarily with such areas as personal preparation for various kinds of positions, preparing credentials, preparing and participating in interviews, and finally the pros and cons of accepting one position as opposed to another.

It is important for both a prospective teacher and a practicing teacher to have some guidelines against which practices can be evaluated so that responsibility may be assumed for self-evaluation of teaching behaviors. This implies that the teacher should develop early a list of principles that can guide him in the evaluation of his practices. There are all sorts of principles with subprinciples given in books and periodicals, but if the individual teacher develops his own set, he is likely to make more use of it to continually improve his practices.

One interesting approach to this problem of principles is described by Selakovich.[1] In the setup suggested, the student teacher begins his list of principles early in his teacher-preparation career. Actually, the list can be started at any time in a professional career. He continues to add to and modify this list of principles, and by the time he is ready for student teaching he is prepared to submit a formal list of principles to the cooperating teacher and his college representative. Such a procedure tends to encourage students and supervisors to really exam-

[1] D. Selakovich, "Self-evaluation by Student Teachers," *Journal of Teacher Education*, 12 (June 1961), pp. 225–228.

ine their beliefs about teaching. It enables the student and the professionals with whom he is working to view teaching in a specific context. Such suggestive lists as those developed by Watson[2] give the prospective teacher or the teacher a useful frame of reference.

Some illustrative items from one social studies teacher are the following:

The teacher should develop in the student a background that will enhance his ability to make intelligent decisions in his daily life.

I believe that the teacher must help the student understand democratic citizenship; that is, he must create a basic understanding in the student of responsibilities and consequences that are needed for democratic citizenship.

The teacher must challenge the student to form his own opinions on important issues, but to first acquire knowledge, to form intelligent opinions; he must challenge his student to look at issues as objectively and open-mindedly as possible.

Good teaching should develop in the student a respect for the individual in a democratic society and an appreciation of the freedoms that our society provides.

Other principles or guidelines suggested by the teacher for his own guidance include some on methods of teaching, the learning situation, attitudes toward the learner, the role of the teacher, and others.

Any list such as the type suggested above will not be completely adequate. However, it will be the professional's own list, and it will help him to give himself an opportunity to test his ideas in a laboratory of direct experience. Such experiences should, of course, be followed up with actual written comments on the success of various types of approaches and with needed revisions of the principles. Such a list can make it easier for others to give help as well as facilitate self-evaluation.

In preparation for a new or different position it is important that the individual recognize the chief problems he is likely to face. For example, a study of the problems that had been listed most frequently by first-year teachers fell into three areas: student-teacher relationships; theory vs. practicality; and administrative problems, including teaching subjects without previous college training in them, lack of equipment, scheduling, and

[2] G. Watson, "What Psychology Can We Feel Sure About?" *Teacher College Record,* **61** (February 1960), pp. 253–257.

finding time for planning. Some crucial questions the teacher needs to raise with himself are: Do I accept criticism on the part of others relative to my own development, or do I resent it? Do I accept myself, my pupils, and my co-workers, or am I dissatisfied with the situation I am in? Satisfaction for the teacher starts with himself, and he must continually attempt to recognize his strengths and weaknesses and try to improve. Am I capable of accepting and respecting the poor, the ADC, the rich, those of other races, those with poor appearance?

In thinking about possible types of positions to consider in the coming year, the teacher or prospective teacher should keep in mind that some positions offer much more opportunity for professional development than others. For example, for the first-year teacher an internship is frequently an excellent way to get off to a good start in teaching with appropriate guidance by others. Some internships pay as much as regular positions, and the teacher is employed with a full-time load and with complete charge of his classes. He, however, gets a certain amount of supervision and help from one or more mature teachers who are given time to work with new teachers in the school system. This person, such as an assistant principal, may be in charge of assisting staff members new to the school system and may work with a nearby college or university from which the intern is a graduate and with whom the graduate is doing advanced work. Under such an arrangement the new teacher can have a wealth of vicarious experiences upon which to fall back. Such organized systematic efforts can help the new instructor meet day-to-day problems in a more effective and satisfying manner. School systems employing the internship program consider the development of human capital as vital to the school and to the individual himself.

A type of different teaching experience that may be very useful to the experienced teacher is sometimes available in teacher-training institutions where the teacher works in a laboratory school with elementary or secondary students part of the time, but during the remaining time he has an opportunity to work with adults and to carry on active research. This type of experience can be very stimulating, professionally, to the experienced teacher. Some school systems also have a teacher exchange program with other systems or with teacher-training institutions.

This approach is frequently well worth investigating when self-evaluation reveals an apparent need for a change in professional scenery.

In enthusiastically supporting and developing strong in-service programs many school systems have followed the lead of farsighted industrial giants who have found that such programs pay in dollars and cents. At IBM, for example, professional workers are urged to average one graduate level course a year as long as they work for the corporation. "General Electric spends $45,000,000 a year . . . to support a curriculum of thousands of courses at dozens of plants across the country with a student body of 35,000."[3] Some educational administrators with vision have decided that the teacher sabbatical may be one of the best investments for education that a community can make. A farsighted school administrator supports continuous professional development not only for new staff members but for veteran teachers as well.

Do I recognize the many varieties of schools and communities? It should be understood that a teacher who may "fail" in one situation may well "succeed" in another. Schools differ greatly in the amount and kind of supervision, in the interpersonal relations among staff members, and in the discipline that exists in the school. Some teachers in deprived areas feel that they may spend as much as three-fourths of their time just in keeping order. Obviously, this is a radically different kind of situation from one where concern with learning is a primary consideration on the part of both pupils and teachers.

The immense variation in the achievement levels of pupils in different schools is well illustrated by the early findings of Project Talent.[4] A comparison of test scores from various parts of the country revealed that students from one school to another showed a great deal of variation in almost every state. Many students in the lowest quarter in the schools which they were currently attending would rank in the highest quarter if attending other schools in the same state. The variation within a particular school is, of course, immense. Flanagan found that in most schools, about 20 per cent of the ninth-grade students

[3] *Time* Magazine, August 28, 1964, p. 44.

[4] J. C. Flanagan, "Early Findings from Project Talent," *NEA Journal*, 53 (January 1964), pp. 8–10.

tested had already attained a higher level of achievement than the average achievement for students in the twelfth grade. This means that the prospective teacher in a school must attempt to be prepared to teach a wide variety of individual ability.

In addition to the variation between schools and the great variation within a particular school in the pupil population we must consider the great differences that exist in communities in the role expected of the teacher. In some communities the teachers are fairly independent citizens who may go about their activities as they see fit. In other communities the citizens expect teachers to conform to rather rigid patterns of behavior. For example, the teacher may be expected to do all of his purchasing in the community that employs him. The teacher may be expected not to smoke or drink or play cards or do many of the other things that other citizens do rather freely.

Within a school the organizational climate may vary greatly. For example, in some schools the newly employed teacher rapidly becomes a part of the teaching team. In other schools, the newcomer may remain an outsider for one, two, or more years. In some schools, overall school evaluation of teaching and learning is attempted. In other schools, teachers look with suspicion upon any colleague who attempts any type of evaluation by students, and such behavior is sometimes viewed as a threat to other teachers. In some schools, the teacher is given his teaching assignment without consultation, and he is expected to carry on. In other schools the principal or department head is very careful to democratically discuss the work assignments of newly employed staff members.

All of the preceding considerations should lead the teacher to ask himself the questions: Is the type of community one in which I would like to work? Also, are the school and the school staff set up in such a way that it is likely I would be happy while working there?

Do I, as a teacher or prospective teacher, recognize that I as a novice may not be able to use some of the techniques that very successful experienced teachers use? As Combs[5] has pointed out:

[5] A. W. Combs, "The Personal Approach to Good Teaching," *Educational Leadership,* **21** (March 1964), pp. 369–377. Copyright © 1964 by the Association for Supervision and Curriculum Development. Reprinted by permission.

. . . it is a fallacy to assume the methods of the experts either can, or should be, taught directly to beginners. It is seldom we can determine what should be for the beginner by examining what the expert does well. I learned this some years ago when I was responsible for teaching failing university students more effective methods of study. At first glance it would seem logical to determine what should be taught to the failing students by determining the study habits of successful ones. Such an approach to curriculum construction, however, is disastrous!

Successful students study more whimsically. They operate without plan, go to the movies often and indulge in all sorts of extra-curricular activities and generally behave in the ways that would be suicidal for students teetering on the brink of failure. It simply does not follow that what is good for the expert is good for the novice too! Nor is it true that the way to become expert is to do what the expert does.

Some of the methods used by the expert can only be used because he is expert. Many experienced teachers have learned to deal with most classroom disturbances by ignoring them. Yet beginners cannot ignore them! The expert is able to ignore matters precisely because he *is* an expert. Some methods cannot even be comprehended without adequate prior experience. One must grow to achieve them. Asking the young teacher to use methods which do not fit him may also turn him loose in the blackboard jungle to fight for his life without appropriate weapons.

Each teacher must assess his own abilities and experience and then attempt to decide what individual approaches are likely to be best *for him.*

Self-evaluation Before and During the Interview

A very important, although too frequently neglected, aspect of seeking a new position is that of preparing credentials carefully and accurately. It is important that the recommendations be requested early of those who are to write them and put on file immediately after a course or other direct contact with the person who is to write the recommendation. Many of those who are writing recommendations deal with hundreds of individuals and after a one- or two-year period it is difficult to recover the impressions that one may have had of a teacher or prospective teacher during contact. Not only should these credentials or recommendations be sought immediately after major contact with an employer or an instructor, but it is very important that credentials be kept up to date even though one is not consciously searching for a new job at a specified time. To keep credentials up to date protects one and gives a type of insurance in that they will be available when needed.

Before going to an interview the following questions may well be used for self-evaluation:

1. Have I learned enough about the school and the community in which I am going to be interviewing, and have I listed questions that I would like to raise with the administrator and/or the teaching committee with whom I am scheduled to talk?

2. Am I prepared to give succinctly my current point of view regarding major educational issues such as discipline, my primary purposes in teaching a particular subject, the roles of the teacher in the classroom, the place of extracurricular activities, the roles of the teacher in working with other teachers, and other similar topics?

3. Have I decided rather specifically what I should say if certain questions are asked such as: Would you accept a contract if I were to offer it to you now? What salary would you expect? Do you believe that teachers should join labor unions? Do you believe that all teachers should belong to the State Education Association? How do you feel about the NEA?

4. What is my attitude toward administrators as a group? This is a question that has not been carefully thought through by many teachers. Willower[6] found that when teacher trainees were asked whether they generally liked or disliked the school administrator, 32 per cent of them volunteered the information that he was sometimes disliked because of his authority, which was resented. When the prospective teachers were asked: "What type of person do you think would like to have a career in school administration?" Sixty-seven per cent pictured the aspirant for administration as a person ambitious for the prestige of high position who sought leadership responsibility. As one student put it, "The person who would really like to be an administrator is probably someone who likes to be boss and run things; someone who is looking for status and who drives to get ahead." The

[6] D. J. Willower, "Education Students' Perceptions of School Administrators," *The School Review,* **70** (Autumn 1962), pp. 332–344.

conscious or unconscious image that the teacher has of administrators is likely to affect not only his initial interview but also the teacher's future professional effectiveness.

Traditionally the administrator has asked all the questions in the interview. Forward-looking administrators as well as teachers are increasingly recognizing that it is important for the teacher to go into a new position with his eyes open to both its challenges and its limitations. Tact in asking questions is, of course, very important. The following questions are illustrative of the types of issues that the teacher may appropriately explore with the administrator in order to make a sensible assessment of working conditions in a prospective position:

1. What arrangements are made for inducting new teachers into the school system? For example, are there workshops prior to the opening of school? If so, who operates these?

2. Is there an active in-service training program during the school year? Is observation of other teachers encouraged? DeVita[7] found that when new teachers observed experienced teachers, when experienced teachers observed experienced teachers, when art teachers observed science teachers, when English teachers observed industrial arts teachers, and when other teachers observed as seemed profitable—all these pairings were found to produce very profitable experiences. The experiences of DeVita as well as other administrators have strongly suggested that observations are profitable not only for the observer but also for the observed in terms of professional development. In the approach described by DeVita, the respect and dignity of each individual teacher were emphasized. The school was not interested in having some teachers sit in judgment on other teachers. Written observation reports concerning the competency of the teacher were not encouraged. No names were used by the observer. No names were to be written on the observation form. The school was not even interested in constructive criticism that might be misconstrued or embarrassing to the teacher. In fact, criticism in any form concerning the work of the teacher was not expected. However, it was found that after five weeks of intervisitation it was almost unanimously declared to be a valuable and worthwhile experience. Such activities may also

[7] J. DeVita, "A Stimulating Technique—Teachers Observe Other Teachers," *The Clearing House*, 37 (May 1963), pp. 549–550.

reflect a very cooperative spirit on the part of various teachers in the system.

3. What is the normal teaching load of beginning instructors? The size of the load, particularly of a beginning teacher, frequently determines his success or failure. Several studies have shown that first-year teachers are generally given heavier loads than more experienced teachers and are sometimes assigned odds and ends, some of which may be subjects outside the teacher's field of preparation.[8] The reason for raising this issue is apparent when it is obvious that an inexperienced teacher is likely to need more time for class preparation, and a reduced or at least not an extra teaching assignment is certainly desirable. However, in many systems across the country the reverse is found where experienced teachers automatically have the first choice of all teaching assignments, and what is left is given to the beginning teachers. It is better to find the answer to the teaching load question before employment rather than after employment.

4. What are nonteaching responsibilities or assignments? In addition to a heavy teaching load, in some school systems the new teacher is given a discouragingly large amount of extra-classroom activity, such as supervision of lunchrooms or halls, bus loading, committee work, school programs, sponsoring of two or more clubs, faculty-meeting preparation. Such activities, while necessary, may so spread the energies of the beginning teacher particularly so that he finds it difficult to accomplish his major classroom duties well.

It is important that the teacher investigate what is expected of him before employment rather than waiting till long after and possibly finding an unfortunate situation. Of course, no teaching situation is ideal. Each position necessarily carries with it some disadvantages. However, both the teacher and the school are likely to profit if the teacher is helped to go into a new position with a fairly adequate appraisal of what he is likely to encounter.

5. Is there a single salary schedule for both elementary and secondary teachers? At what level would I start in the salary scale if I were employed? How much credit is given for out-

[8] R. H. Nelson and M. L. Thompson, "Why Teachers Quit," *The Clearing House,* **37** (April 1963), pp. 467–472.

side services in salary adjustments? What are arrangements for absences? What is the sick pay schedule, and is it cumulative? Are there insurance or other fringe benefits offered by the system? What deductions are made for all regularly employed teachers? In addition to pensions, what are these for?

6. Are there available written descriptions of school practices, including such things as teacher-transfer privileges, pension arrangements, personnel records, responsibilities of department heads, responsibilities of supervisors, responsibilities of principals, arrangements for workshops, and intervisitation possibilities?

7. What are the opportunities and encouragement for professional development and growth on the job? Is there a professional library available for use by teachers? How is work in extramural classes during the school year regarded? How is work in summer school viewed? Is attendance at various professional meetings encouraged or discouraged? What are expectations relative to membership in professional organizations? Is the school currently participating in the tryout of any of the newer curricular materials such as those of the Biological Sciences Curriculum Study,[9] the Foreign Language Instruction Project,[10] the Chemical Bond Approach Project,[11] or materials developed by any of several mathematics programs.[12]

8. Where do most teachers in the system live? What are representative costs? How much privacy does the teacher have in out-of-school hours? What is the distance to appropriate living quarters? Is there any problem of physical safety in the area?

9. Is there a staff evaluation and development program? For example, Sperber[13] has described a significant evaluation and

[9] B. Class, "Renascent Biology: A Report on the AIBS Biological Sciences Curriculum Study," *The School Review,* **70** (Spring 1962), pp. 16–43.

[10] M. A. Riestra and C. E. Johnson, "Changes in Attitudes of Elementary-School Pupils Toward Foreign-Speaking Peoples Resulting from the Study of Foreign Language," *Journal of Experimental Education,* **33** (Fall 1964), pp. 65–72.

[11] L. E. Strong, "Chemistry as a Science in the High School," *The School Review,* **70** (Spring 1962), pp. 44–50.

[12] E. Moise, "The New Mathematics Programs," *The School Review,* **70** (Spring 1962), pp. 82–101.

[13] R. I. Sperber, "A Sound Staff Evaluation Program," *American School Board Journal,* **141** (July 1960), pp. 15–16.

appraisal program which involves three distinct and important stages. The first of these is the preappraisal stage, which involves the selection and orientation of new employees. This serves to set standards of performance. It also gives new employees opportunities in the previous spring and summer to observe and gather needed materials. In the case of employees joining the school system after the beginning of the academic year, opportunities are afforded for observation prior to taking over a position.

Continuous observation with the minimum of three half-hour observations is recommended. On-the-job performance is considered with regard to such factors as (1) personal characteristics, (2) planning and preparation, (3) methods of instructions for work, (4) observable results in people, (5) relationships with others, and (6) attitude toward teaching or work. Each observation of on-the-job performance is followed up with a postobservation conference with an appropriate staff member.

Planning for the yearly appraisal stage with a staff member is the core of the preappraisal stage. The appraiser reviews the employee's record folder; considers results of the postobservation conferences; consults with supervisors or department heads; reexamines lesson plans and/or work schedules; reviews appraisee-pupil relationships; reviews appraisee–co-worker relationships; reviews appraisee-parent relationships; and reviews appraisee-community relationships.

The second stage involves the main appraisal or conference session. The following are characteristic aspects of it:

1. It is set up at a mutually convenient time.
2. The appraiser sets an informal friendly climate for the session.
3. The appraiser develops the appraisee's desire to evaluate his own performance.
4. From this self-evaluation, patterns are traced to indicate the appraisee's area of strength, growth, and possible improvement.
5. An attempt is made to arrive at a common agreement as to the steps needed to make improvement providing a free exchange of ideas.

6. All written points in the appraisal session are summarized. A summary of appraisal remarks is sent to the principal's office.

The third and final stage involves a continual follow-up: checks on the effectiveness of appraisal sessions for growth and general cooperative development for improvement.

Another type of rating of teacher performance for self-improvement is described by Cosgrove.[14] This method presents a procedure for evaluating the relative effectiveness of a teacher's performance in four areas of activities. These areas include:

1. Knowledge and organization of subject matter
2. Adequacy of relations with students in class
3. Adequacy of plans and procedures in class
4. Enthusiasm in working with students

For self-evaluation, phrases descriptive of teacher behavior are grouped, each group representing a phrase from each of the four areas. An advantage of the resulting profile is that the teacher (and his supervisor) can consider his behavior in terms of each of the four dimensions and the behaviors involved. The profile approach with a grouping of items presents an organized and useful analysis of the rating, giving the teacher a clearer idea of his relatively strong and weak areas of performance. The forced-choice arrangement minimizes bias which is so often evidenced in rating schemes. In completing the form, the students rank the phrases in each set as they apply to the instructor. The end result is a profile showing the relative standing of the instructor on the four areas of teacher activity. This type of evaluation approach can be useful not only to the school system but also to the teacher who wants to know where to begin to work on improving his effectiveness.

Finally, after all information the teacher wishes to get or is able to get has been shaken down into the *pros* versus the *cons* for accepting a particular job, an evaluative decision must be

[14] D. J. Cosgrove, "Diagnostic Ratings of Teacher Performance," *Journal of Educational Psychology,* **50** (1959), pp. 200–204.

made. Illustrative of that which some beginning and experienced teachers face, as epitomized by Hunter and Amidon,[15] is the case of Andrea Kern, who wished to teach in the town where she and her husband would be living. She had a fine academic and student teaching record, had been a leader in academic and extracurricular activities, "was a fine musician, a creative person, and one who loved people." She had already been offered two jobs elsewhere but the Northpoint School would be the only one with an opening within twenty-five miles of where she would be living.

As Andrea Kern sized up the situation, the *pros* relative to accepting the job looked something like this:

If this job were not accepted, commuting of over twenty-five miles would be necessary.

"We have a school library. . . . The extent to which the teachers use extra library reading is up to them," said the principal.

The salary was adequate, since her husband would also have a salary.

A second car for which the Kerns would not have the money would not be necessary.

The principal said: "You'll get all the help you need from us. . . ."

The *cons* as Andrea Kern perceived them stacked up like this:

An inspection of the physical setup of the school did not impress her. All classrooms were almost identical, with children's seats "in carefully lined rows with the teacher's desk plunk in the middle of the front of the room."

"The children all stood when they 'recited,' and there was a formal and strict air about the school that didn't appeal to Andrea."

The principal said: "We are primarily interested in basic education. . . . We expect our teachers to be firm disciplinarians, and we don't like frills."

[15] E. Hunter and E. Amidon, *Student Teaching, Cases and Comments* (Chicago: Holt, Rinehart and Winston, 1964), pp. 147–149.

Only one reading series was used, and "we expect every child to have to read through the two books on his grade level before he can progress to the next grade—with an occasional exception, of course."

". . . In the first three grades, we require the reading groups to meet twice each day; once in the morning and once in the afternoon. We use the view-and-learn phonics system, and this is particularly stressed in the first two grades. And we do insist on three groups in reading. We have found that there is simply not adequate time for more than that if each child is to receive enough drill." (This shook Andrea up a bit, since there had been a great deal of freedom in the two places where she had done student teaching and there had been three or four basal reading series, as well as extensive library reading. Also the groups did not even have to meet once a day, let alone twice, if the teacher considered other activities more important. In the other schools reading was viewed as an integral part of the school day—and as a tool, not an end in itself.)

"Social studies" was divided into two distinct parts—history three times a week and geography twice. A strict time schedule for teaching all units was set up in advance, and Andrea would be expected to follow it closely if she accepted the job. (This depressed Andrea, since "she was used to an emerging curriculum, within broad guidelines, and she was used to having the day flow as seemed appropriate according to the content and the children, not according to some predetermined time schedule.")

The work sounded more clerical than creative.

The principal said: ". . . but you will have to accommodate yourself to us, and not expect our system to fit you."

Should Andrea Kern accept the position?

How does limiting oneself, as Andrea was, affect the teacher? The teaching profession?

How autonomous should the teacher be in making certain kinds of decisions in his classroom?

In what areas is it reasonable to expect the teacher "to accommodate" himself to the school system? In what areas should the system accommodate to the teacher?

4

Knowledge and Teacher Self-evaluation

THE CRITERIA of teacher effectiveness must be directly related to changes in students. One major dimension of these changes must certainly be in the field of knowledge and cognitive processes. Changes or learnings in this area are ones that teachers emphasize continually in their classroom activities, including assigning work, testing, and a host of other behaviors.

In view of the great emphasis appropriately attached to the development of knowledge in the pupil, it seems reasonable to assume that the teacher himself should give major consideration to his own knowledge, including its current status and particularly its growth. The problem faced by the modern teacher in keeping his knowledge current is particularly challenging. The knowledge explosion, which is resulting in a doubling of knowledge in many fields in about a ten-year period, makes it imperative that the alert teacher examine systematic ways of keeping his own knowledge up to date. It seems obvious that a teacher who has permitted himself to slip farther and farther back in terms of his own knowledge is not in a very good position to encourage youngsters to learn and keep abreast of current knowledge in appropriate fields.

The teacher who does not continually learn himself will slip backward for two primary reasons. First, there is the well-known factor of forgetting. Only a minor fraction of what was learned three or four years before is likely to be remembered by the teacher. The second major factor that should cause the teacher to be concerned is that new knowledge is continually supplanting the old. What was believed twenty years ago in many fields is no longer considered the best available information. Education that is good and proper in teacher training is sufficient only if it includes ways of renewing and rethinking that knowledge that has already been learned. A third major factor that makes increased knowledge of major importance is that if the teacher is to set an example to students of learning, he, himself, must continually be learning and improving. Youngsters are fairly sharp, and if they recognize that while the teacher *talks* about the importance of increasing knowledge but he does not really believe in it sufficiently to keep himself up to date, then the youngsters are likely to feel the teacher is attempting to tell them to do something that he, himself, does not really believe.

How Can the Teacher Make a Self-assessment of His Knowledge?

In most fields there is a wealth of test material which the teacher can acquire and through which he can examine himself. These tests, published by major test companies, cover all of the major fields and can give the teacher leads on what national experts think is important and should be emphasized. Possibly the best single source for test listings is *Tests in Print*,[1] which presents a comprehensive bibliography of 2,126 different test entries and includes such major classifications as mathematics, English, reading, social studies, science, foreign languages, business education, achievement batteries, and fine arts. A study by Vander Werf presents evidence that a relationship exists between what a teacher knows about his special field and his succcess in teaching. Vander Werf also points out that it is nearly impossible to gain mastery in a certain field during a four-year tenure in college.[2]

Another of the better sources for such materials is the *Mental Measurement Yearbooks*,[3] which give some reviews of recent

[1] O. K. Buros, *Tests in Print* (Highland Park, N.J.: The Gryphon Press, 1961).

[2] L. S. Vander Werf, *How to Evaluate Teachers and Teaching* (New York: Rinehart and Co., 1958).

[3] O. K. Buros (ed.), *The Fourth Mental Measurements Yearbook* and *The Fifth Mental Measurements Yearbook* (Highland Park, N.J.: The Gryphon Press, 1953 and 1959).

tests in each field and also give a fairly complete listing of the achievement tests in various fields. Table 1 indicates the number of achievement tests listed in the two most recent yearbooks.

After getting sample or specimen tests, which are usually very inexpensive, the teacher can self-administer the test and interpret his own achievement using the norms. This is good experience as a check on his own self-knowledge and also to acquire additional familiarity with test manuals and norms and to prepare himself to construct better tests for his own students. For example, the foreign language teacher might get and take several of the 40 tests listed in the *Fifth Mental Measurements Yearbook*.[4] The English teacher could well consider examining some of the reviews of English, composition, and literature tests in the same yearbook. He might then get and take personally some of the 47 tests listed in the yearbook in these areas. The elementary and secondary teacher of science or mathematics might, himself, very appropriately take some of the "modern" mathematics or science tests which reflect both the newer trends of experts in the field and revised organization of such knowledge. One example of write-ups of newer trends in these fields is included in the *School Review* for spring 1962.[5] Some trends in the modern renascence in biology, chemistry, and mathematics for both the elementary and the secondary fields are described and reviewed. Additional sources are also given which can help the teacher.

Instructors in these and other fields have found it an exhilarating and challenging experience to see what changes have taken place in materials since they studied in college.

Still another source the teacher can use in diagnosing his knowledge strengths and weaknesses is the National Teachers Examination, which about two hundred schools and about four hundred teacher-training institutions either require or encourage their teacher candidates to take. Indiana and Vermont encourage their teachers to use the NTE for their own professional development, and South Carolina uses NTE scores for certification. The NTE has two basic types of tests: The Common Examination "covers fields of professional information, English

---

[4] *Ibid.*
[5] Volume **70**, pp. 1–147.

TABLE 1

Number of Achievement Tests Listed in Various Fields*

	1953	1959
Achievement batteries	26	21
English tests	30	31
Composition tests	2	4
Literature tests	18	12
Spelling tests	15	11
Vocabulary tests	16	9
Art tests	6	1
Music tests	6	12
Foreign language tests	34	40
General mathematics tests	15	24
Algebra tests	18	18
Arithmetic tests	24	38
Geometry tests	17	10
Trigonometry tests	3	1
Agriculture tests	2	—
Business education tests	21	26
Etiquette tests	4	3
Health tests	13	16
Home economics tests	12	5
Industrial arts tests	2	4
Philosophy tests	2	1
Psychology tests	3	3
Religious education tests	3	5
Listening comprehension	—	2
Safety education tests	5	3
Reading tests	50	72
Study skills tests	11	13
Science tests	7	17
Biology tests	11	11
Chemistry tests	16	19
General science tests	7	—
Geology tests	1	1
Miscellaneous science tests	2	—
Physics tests	11	11
Social studies tests	8	15
Economics tests	4	1
Geography tests	5	6
History tests	19	35
Political science tests	10	—
Sociology tests	2	3
Specific vocations (chiefly achievement tests)	31	50
Speech	—	2
Handwriting	—	2

* From O. K. Buros (ed.), *The Fourth Mental Measurements Yearbook* and *The Fifth Mental Measurements Yearbook* (Highland Park, N.J.: The Gryphon Press, 1953 and 1959).

expression, social studies, literature, fine arts, science and mathematics, nonverbal reasoning. Optional examinations are available in the following fields: education in the elementary school; early childhood education; biology and general science; English language and literature; industrial arts education; mathematics; chemistry, physics, and general science; social studies; physical education; business education; and music education."[6]

Another avenue the teacher may employ in assessing his own knowledge or others' perception of his own knowledge in the fields in which he is teaching is to give a questionnaire to his students which can give the teacher some feedback on how the students perceive his knowledge. Some illustrative items for which anonymous responses may be requested follow:[7]

A. *Open-Ended Illustrations*

   In comparing the teacher in this class with other teachers you are now having:
   a. To what extent would you say he knows the subject matter of the course?
   b. How extensive would you say his cultural background is?
   The instructor's knowledge was best illustrated in which part(s) of the course?
   In which area(s) do you feel the instructor's knowledge is possibly weak?
   The teacher seems to have much information on:
   The teacher seems to know little about:

B. *Checklist Illustrations* (Check items that apply to the instructor of this class.)

   Instructor: ____ sticks close to book; ____ has to look at textbook to answer questions raised by students; ____ often says: "look it up yourself"; ____ rarely makes suggestions about where to get additional information on subject; ____ suggests many new and stimulating ideas about subject studied; ____ gives appropriate, adequate, and challenging answers to questions; ____ shows evidence of broad cultural background; ____ fails to enrich discussions with illustrations from related areas; ____ knows subject matter but has strong prejudices in favor of some aspects; ____ appears to have serious gaps in his knowledge of subject matter in course area; ____ tries to

---

[6] Vander Werf, *op. cit.*

[7] Adapted from R. H. Simpson and J. M. Seidman, "Illustrative Items for Teacher Self-Evaluative Instruments," *Student Evaluation of Teaching and Learning* (Washington, D.C.: The American Association of Colleges for Teacher Education, 1962).

bluff when he doesn't know the facts; ____ knows the field well enough but frequently goes off on tangents.

C. *Rating-Scale Illustrations* (Check the option in each question that best applies to the instructor of this class.)

To what extent does the work of the instructor impress you as indicating mastery in the field of this course?
____very markedly
____markedly
____average
____little
____very little

Instructor's preparation for class session:
____frequently forgets teaching materials
____obviously unprepared
____apparently does a minimum of preparation
____well prepared
____outstanding

Instructor's knowledge of subject:
____seems to know the subject extremely well
____knows the subject well
____seems moderately well informed
____appears to be poorly informed

Instructor's knowledge of where to find information in his field:
____very broad
____adequate
____rather weak
____very weak

How much evidence is there that the instructor has broad experience in his field aside from book knowledge?
____frequent evidence
____fair amount of evidence
____a little evidence
____no evidence

A list such as the preceding can be considered raw material from which the teacher can construct his own questionnaire against the background of his own teaching goals and procedures. The teacher can then assess student perception of him and his knowledge. It is quite possible that students may be very wrong in their perceptions. However wrong these perceptions of students may be, they are important if the teacher is to have desirable relationships with his students. Sometimes the problem is one of inappropriate communication between teacher and students. When a student asks a question, the teacher may ask another question in an attempt to get the student to think.

Unless care is taken, the student may mistakenly conclude the teacher does not *know* the answer to his question. New data from such evaluations can be compared with those which were kept on file from earlier classes. Differences can give important clues to improvements needed or accomplished.

Another type of knowledge the teacher can ill afford to neglect is that given by research results relative to pupil learning. For example, a study by Thompson and Hunnicutt[8] suggests:

1. Either praise or blame is more effective in increasing the work output of fifth-grade pupils than no external incentives.
2. If repeated often enough, praise increases the work output of introverts until it is significantly higher than that of introverts who are blamed or extroverts who are praised.
3. If repeated often enough, blame increases the work output of extroverts until it is significantly higher than that of extroverts who are praised or introverts who are blamed.

This study suggests the need for not only knowledge of research results but also knowledge of some key personality characteristics of each learner. Without such knowledge teacher behavior may be unwise.

How Can the Teacher Use the Results of Self-assessment of His Knowledge?

New advances are being developed in a great variety of fields. Their importance cannot be overemphasized for the teacher. Some implications are summarized by Chase.[9]

No one can follow the evolution of the curriculum projects in biology, physics, mathematics, and chemistry without becoming aware of the fact that, taken as a whole, these studies incorporate philosophical concepts and have radical implications for educational objectives, curriculum theory, the practice of teaching, and the organization and administration of schools. Consciously or unconsciously, and more or less consistently, the studies reflect emerging, though not yet

[8] G. G. Thompson and C. W. Hunnicutt, "The Effect of Repeated Praise or Blame on the Work Achievement of 'Introverts' and 'Extroverts,'" *Journal of Educational Psychology*, 35 (May 1944), pp. 257–266.

[9] F. S. Chase, "Some Effects of Current Curriculum Projects on Educational Policy and Practices," *The School Review*, 70 (Spring 1962), pp. 132–147. Reprinted by permission of The University of Chicago Press and F. S. Chase.

clearly enunciated, concepts of the nature of man and how he learns, and of the nature of knowledge and its uses.[10]

With regard to a theory of knowledge, the curriculum studies are grounded in a view that rejects the notion of specific items of information to be learned and the view that extension of knowledge occurs through a simple process of accretion. In the proposed organizations of the curriculum, all pretense of covering the field of knowledge is abandoned, and reliance is placed instead on apprehension of the system of basic concepts and their logical consequences. These concepts serve, not only as a structure for holding related bits of knowledge but also as perspectives through which to view phenomena —perspectives moreover that are recognized as partial and temporary in nature and therefore to be supplemented and/or replaced in time by other perspectives.[11]

This revised concept of the nature of knowledge and what should be taught has profound implications for the teacher, his own knowledge, and the kind of knowledge he attempts to teach to his pupils. The modern view of knowledge recognizes not only that new facts are being added to our granary of knowledge but even more important that knowledge is constantly being reorganized so that our hope of keeping up with advancing knowledge requires the ability to rethink what has already been learned rather than merely to add to what the individual knows. As Chase states, "The process is one in which new conceptions give rise to new perceptions and heightened perceptions in turn eventuate in new concepts."[12]

Results from new curricula show "that most children enjoy them and show marked aptitude for learning with them. But it must be noted that the dramatic results that have been reported usually involve instruction by teachers who are thoroughly grounded in the subject they are teaching. . . . However, few of today's innovations have been fully developed and tested."[13] Sound participation in curricular innovations demands new knowledge on the part of the teacher.

The good teacher can never be satisfied with his current knowledge, for as Whitehead[14] says, the ideas we deal with

[10] *Ibid.*, p. 132.

[11] *Ibid.*, p. 134.

[12] *Ibid.*, p. 135.

[13] G. Heathers, "The Role of Innovation in Education," *The National Elementary Principal*, **43** (September 1963), pp. 9–14.

[14] A. N. Whitehead, *Science in the Modern World* (New York: The Macmillan Company, 1925), p. 186.

"are never static. They are either fading into meaningless formulae, or are gaining power by the new lights thrown by more delicate apprehension."

There are many avenues open to the teacher who wants to keep his organization of knowledge up to date. Many institutions offer extramural classes in various centers which can be taken, even by full-time teachers. Correspondence courses are frequently an avenue whereby the teacher can, as time permits, keep himself somewhat abreast of current developments in some of the fields he teaches.

Workshops and in-service institutes for English teachers, elementary education teachers, music teachers, and many other fields are available. In the years 1953 to 1960 over 80,000 teachers enrolled in summer, academic-year, and in-service institutes for teaching of science, mathematics, and engineering.

The initiation of an active faculty professional library can be a way that a faculty committee or administrator can encourage improved professional growth. Setting up a system of rotating new materials as they come in so that each faculty member has a chance to examine each of the new materials can lead to improved knowledge on the part of the staff. Faculty in-service training programs can be a vital stimulant to the teacher who wishes to keep professionally alive and up to date in knowledge and concepts important in his field.

5

Self-evaluation in Developing
Goals and Procedures

BECAUSE OF THE NATURE of his work the teacher is de-
nied clear-cut measures of effectiveness of his goals and procedures. However, in order to have the best assessment of efficiency possible it is necessary that personal goals and procedures
be carefully analyzed. Clear-cut goals are needed for two primary reasons: first, as a basis for evaluation and, second, to give
direction to teaching.

There are several questions the teacher can appropriately
use in considering goals in relation to his teaching.

Do I have too similar goals for all students? The range of
five to ten average grade levels of ability in a particular class is,
of course, not uncommon. However, the implied goals of many
teachers with such classes make it appear that this actual
range is completely disregarded. Even with so-called homogeneous grouping there are many differences. For example,
Golber[1] describes a group assembled to learn to read. They
were grouped on the basis of their grade levels as shown by a
standardized test which indicated all had a 4.5 grade level. However,

. . . student *A* is in 3a and is brilliant. Student *B* is in his normal
grade. *C* is in the sixth grade and guesses as to word identity, mis-
taking "tuck" for "truck." *D* is in seventh grade and has mastered the

[1] L. M. Golber, "Grade Level Tests: A Smear and a Delusion?" *Chicago Schools Journal,* **43** (February 1962), pp. 215–218. Reprinted by permission.

mechanics of reading but being a recent immigrant has an inadequate vocabulary. *E* has an excellent speaking vocabulary but has brain damage which prevents him from comprehending print easily. *F* is partially deaf. Or consider an arithmetic class, grade 5.0, grouped by grade level as is determined by standardized tests. Mary does not know her addition facts; Jerry is confused about "borrowing"; Kenneth does not understand division by fractions; and Marlene has a fixed idea that 7×8 is 58. It is apparent that the "homogeneity" is spurious and utterly misleading.

Popular opinion about "ability grouping" is frequently erroneous. After a careful study of research evidence, Shores[2] concluded "the real problem, then, is caring for individual differences, and the more effective the instruction, the greater the heterogeneity of the group. Hence, if we group, we must regroup often; and whether we group or not is of much less concern than whether we care for the differences within each group." "Homogeneous grouping" does not make all individuals in a class the same. It would be as easy to group members of a class in terms of physical appearance as it is to group them in terms of mental ability and personal characteristics important in learning various school activities.

Do I pay too little attention to the goal of reading improvement? The modern idea of reading is that one should continue to learn to read as long as he continues to learn anything through reading; also one never becomes a completely proficient reader and must continually develop the complex skills and abilities involved in various subjects. Reading is important for all teachers, since reading instruction isolated from science, English, mathematics, or any other reading subjects is carried on for the most part in a vacuum. Many of the student weaknesses shown in science, mathematics, social studies, and other subjects are due to student ineffectiveness in reading *that particular subject.* The effective teacher in each of these subjects must take this into account and be a teacher of reading. Such books as *The Improvement of Reading* by Ruth Strang *et al.* and *Making Better Readers* by Ruth Strang and Dorothy Bracken[3] can be

[2] J. H. Shores, "What Does Research Say About Ability Grouping by Classes?" *Illinois Education,* **27** (December 1964), pp. 169–172.

[3] R. Strang *et al., The Improvement of Reading* (New York: McGraw-Hill Book Co., 1961); R. Strang and D. Bracken, *Making Better Readers* (Boston: D. C. Heath & Co., 1957).

helpful to the teacher who is willing to accept the challenge of poor reading in his subject and attempt to help students develop better reading habits rather than simply wailing to other teachers that his students cannot read. The reading of formulas and symbols in mathematics requires a different set of skills from the reading in a history book which seeks to trace the causes of historical events.

Have I analyzed my teaching goals as indicated by the tests I have used? Tests are the best single mirrors of teacher goals. Students tend to judge course and class emphases and goals by the kinds of test questions they encounter. Involvement of students in the construction of tests can be a useful way to help students participate in the setting of goals and in the development of their own thought-through goals. Many of the so-called intangibles can be measured if they have been carefully defined and described in behavioral terms.

Not only do tests reflect goals but they also suggest which procedures are most effective. For example, a three-year study in the New York City school system indicates those who were taught in language laboratories did far better in language fluency, intonation, and listening comprehension than those who were taught solely by conventional methods. In vocabulary, grammar, and reading comprehension both groups did equally well.[4]

Do I give sufficient attention to the development of student independence and creativity? The vast range of individual differences typically found in the classroom can never be adequately met unless we enlist the active support of each pupil in helping to set his own goals and objectives. It is impossible for the teacher to do an adequate job of continually setting and revising the goals for each individual; and the sooner we recognize this, the more rapid will be our development in helping students generate appropriate goals of their own.

Two main questions may be raised by the teacher who is attempting to diagnose ways of improving creativity in the classroom. The first of these is to diagnose the types of activities that are to be avoided, since they tend to develop liability learnings, conformity, and lack of creativity. The second is to decide on

---

[4] *Education Digest,* **28** (December 1962), p. 45.

positive approaches one may emphasize to encourage independence and creativity.

A group of teachers when faced with what to avoid and a
consideration of their own current behaviors arrived at the following list:

1. Avoid encouraging students to depend on the teacher to
   get all learning processes under way.
2. Avoid having the teacher make all tests and all diagnoses.
3. Avoid having the teacher decide exclusively what is to be
   studied, how it is to be studied, and when it is to be
   studied.
4. Avoid having the teacher exclusively select all materials.
5. Avoid having the teacher set all standards.
6. Avoid attempting to have the teacher provide all motivation.
7. Avoid telling students to study whether or not they see
   any reason for study.

A single teacher in analyzing his own weaknesses suggested
the following items for areas of avoidance:

1. I like to monopolize the class time in lecturing.
2. I get impatient with learner mistakes and slowness.
3. I excuse weaknesses by the compensating device of be-
   lieving that present-day students do not know or care to
   take responsibility or initiative. I discourage students
   by too great a percentage of condemnation over praise.
4. I fail to enlist the pupil in work through his seeing the
   need for it.
5. I justify the lack of development of creativity and learner
   responsibility by thinking that it is uneconomical in time
   and effort, and I need to realize that economy may not
   mean actual learning that will last and be used.
6. I fail to recognize that students must be given the opportunity to make some mistakes if they are to develop self-
   responsibility and initiative.

What activities must be encouraged if members of the class
are to develop creativity and self-responsibility?

Rubin[5] suggests "the valid creative situation requires a reasonable respect for the following: active taking-hold of a problem; a self-directed, sustained effort to discover its solution; and an appraisal of the solution's worth." A group of teachers concerned with developing learner initiative and creativity in their classrooms decided:

1. They would permit students to help choose problems more under the criterion of worthwhileness.
2. They would help learners plan their work more in accordance with their present and future needs and interests. More attempt would be made to relate individual student goals and class goals to out-of-school problems and conditions.
3. They would attempt to encourage increasing self-dependence and decreasing teacher guidance as a semester or a year went past.
4. They would use a great variety of procedures rather than a single standard procedure. For example, they would make more use of pretests for determining levels of readiness in connection with each particular course.
5. They would use much more teacher-pupil planning by means of student committees and teacher-pupil interaction in setting up assignments.
6. They would have more subgroup activities based on interest.
7. They would use more pupil leadership.
8. They would give more consideration to individual differences in interests, abilities, purposes, and so on.
9. They would make more use of informal procedures in planning work with students.
10. They would make more use of unit or long-term assignments as opposed to daily assignments.
11. They would make more use of student self-evaluation activities.
12. They would make more use of many sensory approaches including television, radio, interviews out of school, original compositions.

[5] L. J. Rubin, "Creativeness in the Classroom," *Journal of Secondary Education*, **30** (March 1963), pp. 187–191.

13. They would allow for more differentiated areas and levels of learning activity within a particular class.

14. They would make more use of materials and activities at all levels of ability and in all levels of interest represented in their classes.

15. They would put greater stress on reflective, judgmental, and decision-making activities on the part of learners.

16. They would give more encouragement to students to keep individual records of their own needs and purposes.

17. They would guide learner activities rather than try to dictate them.

Self-evaluation of one's own creativity is important for the teacher who is attempting to teach creativity and self-responsibility on the part of students. After much study of psychological aspects of creative thinking and problem solving, Guilford[6] concluded:

At all stages of problem solving, evaluated abilities contribute to the selection of the best information and the rejection of unsuitable information. The initial step of sensing a problem is itself an active evaluation, as is the final step of accepting a finished product. At any step of the way, evaluation provides guiding influences, although there are times when judgments should be relaxed for the sake of idea production in a large quantity.

Creativity and independence can be taught to students by having the teacher, himself, be creative and independent in his activities. "If a girl can learn more German by reading alone in the janitor's storage room, why keep her in the classroom?" This is the question raised by Asbell[7] who says it is being done. Students are studying, independent of classroom instruction, in what was the janitor's storage room at Melbourne High School, Florida, near Cape Kennedy.

A seventeen-year-old honors student came to B. Frank Brown, Principal at Melbourne High School, asking permission to drop her major subject, German, in which she had been earning A's. Eager to

[6] J. P. Guilford, "Three Faces of Intellect," *American Psychologist,* **14** (1959), pp. 469–479.

[7] B. Asbell, "High School of Sky High Learning," *The Education Digest,* **29** (March 1964), pp. 26–28. The excerpt that follows is reprinted by permission of *The Education Digest.*

read German poetry and plays, she was trapped as the class kept drilling in sentence structure and vocabulary that she had mastered.

Brown told the girl to stay away from class except for exams. He installed her in a corner of the janitor's storage room, supplied her with books of German poetry and plays, and arranged for her to meet her teachers twice a week. Her interest in German soared.

Principal Brown began taking applications from other ambitious students who wished to pursue independent scholarship in a janitor storage room. The room soon became so crowded that Brown tacked a sign, "center for advanced study," on the locked door and issued keys to qualified students. A key to the room soon became a badge of membership in the school's most exclusive and respected club. This year, from a 2,000 total enrollment, more than 100 students have "escaped forward" to enjoy the excitement of self-propelled, self-reliant learning. "The slowest student in this school as well as the brightest one," says Brown, "is capable of things we never dreamed he could do. Both are slowed down because they are prisoners of each other in lock step education. We keep hearing about the miracles at Cape Kennedy. There are more miracles in the potential of young minds than all the scientific miracles at the Cape."

To break the lock step Brown has rebuilt the academic program around the ability of the student rather than his grade in school, making Melbourne High School the only completely nongraded high school in the United States. There are many difficulties in the transition.

While the difficulties were staggering, Brown and his teachers were willing to accept the challenge and meet and use individual differences.

The significance of Melbourne's program can partially be judged by the fact that five years ago only 40 per cent of Melbourne's graduates entered college. The figure is now 73 per cent. These figures are important but Principal Brown says, "These are measures of achievement. But the whole idea of our school is to cultivate imagination and creativity. These are often confused with achievements but are not the same things. Einstein used to preach that imagination is far more important than knowledge, and that's our byword."

The importance of teacher self-commitment to creative thinking is shown in a study by Myers and Torrance.[8] They concluded that those teachers who were least successful were ones who did not value personally the goal of creative thinking. They were

[8] R. E. Myers and E. P. Torrance, "Can Teachers Encourage Creative Thinking?" *Educational Leadership,* **19** (December 1961), pp. 156–160.

authoritarian, defensive, dominated by time, insensitive to pupils' intellectual and emotional needs, lacking in energy, preoccupied with their information-giving functions, intellectually inert, disinterested in promoting initiative and self-reliance in their pupils, preoccupied with disciplinary matters, and unwilling to give much of themselves.

Some teachers and administrators may be fearful of encouraging creativity because they may doubt their own abilities to deal with it. Creative people are often designated as "characters" or "troublemakers." However, if we encourage pupils to think and analyze and evaluate, we must expect that they are going to come up with some ideas that are at variance with our ideas.

Have I analyzed the postschool behavioral goals I am shooting for? One of the best ways to attempt to pinpoint behavioral objectives is to consider this: In what way would I hope that these students would behave differently after they are out of school as a result of what I have been teaching them? This phrasing of the problem tends to help the teacher avoid exclusively generalized objectives such as developing appreciation or developing understanding.

Have I analyzed activities during the first class session? A group of teachers after carefully listing and considering individual differences and psychological principles as they might be applied to teaching came up with the following suggestions on the way they felt their first class session would probably differ from what they had previously done.

1. They would entertain learner suggestions more for class activities and projects.
2. They would explain general procedures and give more attention to developing class objectives with learners.
3. They would tend to guide rather than completely dominate planning activities.
4. They would spend more time securing personal data from students in questionnaires and from the office, including results of tests that had been taken previously.
5. They would do more interviewing of learners with respect to their interests and purposes and in some cases would use questionnaires to get at this.

6. They would encourage more learner responsibility in connection with the planning of assignments. They would try to make the class "our" class rather than the "teacher's" class.

7. They would give more consideration in seating and in other regard to those who might be physically handicapped. For example, the hard of hearing, the nearsighted, the left-handed, and others would be given special attention in seating and in assignment making.

8. Assignments would always be given in written form to the hard of hearing.

Have I diagnosed my questioning and verbal interaction? Modern curriculum experts tend to reject the older view that extension of knowledge occurs through a simple process of accretion of specific items of information to be learned. Chase,[9] for example, indicates:

Under the new view the selection of content becomes not so much a matter of identifying the aspects of knowledge deemed of most worth as of identifying the concepts that will be most fruitful in advancing understanding and the pursuit of new knowledge. These illuminating and fructifying concepts in a given field of knowledge are then to be presented with sufficient illustrative and speculative detail to permit their apprehension and use. In organizing content the aim is to enable the learner to proceed from initial grasp of a concept to more comprehensive understandings and applications, and to perceive the interrelationships among the basic concepts. The content of the learning experience embodies, not only the concepts themselves and the implications that flow from them, but also the ways in which concepts are developed and tested for cogency and effectiveness, how they contribute over a shorter or longer period to the enhancement of knowledge, and how they are modified or replaced in the light of subsequent investigations. This view takes account not only of the rapid expansion of knowledge but also, and more important, of the fact that knowledge is constantly being reorganized and reconstituted, so that man's hope of keeping up with advancing knowledge requires the ability to rethink what he has already learned rather than merely add to what he knows.

[9] F. S. Chase, "Some Effects of Current Curriculum Projects on Educational Policy and Practices," *The School Review*, **70** (Spring 1962), pp. 134–135. Reprinted by permission of The University of Chicago Press and F. S. Chase.

In this modern approach the role of verbal interaction and questioning becomes very important. Some of the issues which the teacher needs to consider are suggested in the following questions:

1. How will it be determined whether the instructor is really communicating with students effectively?
2. How should the proportion of time spent in one-way communication, as opposed to two-way communication, be determined?
3. In a particular subject, how should the number of times the instructor speaks in relation to the number of times students talk differ?
4. How should the total amount of talk of students compare with the amount of talk by the instructor?
5. To what extent should the teacher's talking as opposed to the student's talking structure class discussions?
6. To what extent should the teacher encourage students to clarify questions asked?
7. To what extent should students be encouraged to express their views, particularly when these views are in conflict with course readings or the teacher's personal views?
8. What should be the teacher's behavior when a student asks a question; should he answer it or use it as a sounding board for getting other students to think?
9. To what extent should the teacher incorporate the students' remarks, suggestions, desires, or criticisms into the structuring and direction of the class?
10. To what extent should the teacher attempt to recognize and reorganize the class dynamics in terms of who speaks and how often?
11. To what extent should the problems discussed be an outgrowth of student needs and/or perceptions of what is important?
12. To what extent should the discussion provide an opportunity to determine the congruence of teacher's views and individual students' perceptions on a problem?
13. To what extent should the teacher take active steps to make the class group aware of structuring problems in the class and problems of class dynamics?

Making sound recordings of lessons taught by 38 teachers and transcribed for analysis, Jayne,[10] after analyzing 184 items that were observable in the classroom, found 11 items that showed some promise of significance. These were combined into scales called the Index of Meaningful Discussion and the Index of Immediate Recall. The former contained the following seven items:

1. Per cent of fact questions on unprepared material
2. Per cent of thought questions on unprepared material
3. Per cent of thought questions dealing with local situations
4. Number of participations growing out of spontaneous pupil discussion
5. Number of teacher explanations
6. Number of times teacher presented factual information
7. Times teacher raised a question as to correctness of a pupil response

The Index of Immediate Recall contained four items:

1. Questions demanding recall of specified facts
2. Number of factual questions on prepared material
3. Number of thought questions on prepared material
4. Number of times teacher indicated answer right

A description of how the type of analysis just indicated affected one teacher may be helpful.[11] In a teacher workshop or lab studying class interactions a particular high school English teacher at the beginning of the lab told staff members that no education courses ever helped him and the only way for a teacher to improve his efficiency was to increase his understanding of the subject matter which he was teaching.

Each participant in the laboratory had brought with him a tape recording of 30 minutes of his own classroom interaction. It was the systematic analysis of this tape recording that first made this high school English teacher question his attitude toward teaching. The analysis of this particular teacher's interaction pattern unearthed the following facts:

1. Fifty per cent of the total classroom interaction was teacher questioning, lecturing, and giving directions.

[10] C. D. Jayne, "A Study of the Relationship Between Teaching Procedures and Educational Outcomes," *The Journal of Experimental Education,* 14 (1945), pp. 101–134. The excerpts that follow are reprinted by permission.

[11] E. Amidon, I. Casper, and B. Shantz, "Self-Analysis of Teaching Techniques," *Pennsylvania School Journal,* 112 (October 1963), pp. 65–66. The excerpt that follows is reprinted by permission.

2. Less than 10 per cent of the teacher talk was encouragement or acceptance of students' ideas.
3. Less than 20 per cent of the total classroom interaction was classified as student talk.
4. Over 70 per cent of the total interaction in the classroom was teacher talk.
5. Over 80 per cent of the student talk followed a teacher question, direction, or criticism.
6. Less than 35 per cent of the questions asked by the teacher were answered or responded to by the students.

This information was important because it gave this particular teacher some basic facts about his own classroom behavior. These facts, although they do not represent an unusual pattern, surprised this teacher because he had thought of himself as a different kind of teacher—a teacher who talked little, used student ideas, and encouraged much spontaneous student participation.

This teacher has tried to make some changes in the way he interacts with children in the classroom. He has used some tools of research to analyze the present situation; he has developed some hypotheses about what he might do differently and what effects his behavior change would have; he has set up specific plans or steps to take in his classroom; and he has begun to take action and plans to collect more data later to evaluate the success of his change in behavior.

It is clear that the advantages of this kind of procedure are that the teacher can evaluate research findings in terms of his own classroom behavior; he can try out ideas and evaluate their success by collecting data in his own classroom.

By doing this, the teacher can gain insight into his own behavior and into the behavior of his class and can be encouraged to formulate his own individual theory of teacher behavior. In a final analysis we know that this is the only kind of theory that can have real meaning for him.

Modern devices make it possible for the teacher to diagnose his classroom behavior. Sound recorders, sound films, cameras and projectors, kinescopes, video tape recorders, and playbacks all have great promise for the teacher who wishes to analyze and improve his instruction.

Have I used self-evaluation of class goals and procedures to help on discipline? The disciplinary aspect of a class is, itself, an indirect type of diagnosis. Poor discipline still rates at the top of practically every list of teaching problems. Poor discipline is basically a reflection, a symptom, of some underlying difficulties that the teacher has not successfully faced. These difficulties may be in the nature of the assignments, in lack of attention to individual differences, in inappropriate or insufficient variety in texts, or in class procedures.

We want, of course, to develop self-motivated, self-guided individuals, since the eventual test of education will take place when teachers are no longer around to prod, to direct, and to make decisions for the learner. Self-responsibility and self-guidance come only through permitting the student much decision making, which will inevitably involve some mistakes on his part.

There are various techniques that the teacher may use in getting at possible causes of disciplinary problems. The nine questions given below were devised "to bring to light the facts regarding the fulfillment of the teacher's responsibility in a particular teaching situation."[12] It will be noted that the questions to be answered by the teacher deal with procedures, behavior, attitude, method, and time budgeting as well as the day-to-day condition of the teacher.

Form for Self-Analysis of Classroom Teaching

This instrument is designed to be used daily over a period of several weeks. It might be the basis for conferences between the teacher and supervisory personnel.

1. What procedures or devices used in this lesson were effective?
2. What procedures were ineffective?
3. What personal mannerisms or attitudes were apparent to the class which were not desirable?
4. What overt signs of misbehavior, if any, were present? Who were the pupils directly involved?
5. To what causes, either of the teaching or the personalities of the pupils involved, can this misbehavior be attributed?
6. What signs, if any, were there that certain pupils were doing exceptionally good work? Who were these pupils?
7. What sort of a day am I having? Is there anything causing me to be tense, worried, or fatigued?
8. Was the major objective of my lesson reached? Did the pupils grasp the idea or ideas presented? If not, why not?
9. Were lesson plans and preparation adequate? Was my time well assigned?[13]

A mathematics teacher who had been having a large amount of trouble with student discipline to the extent that the class

---

[12] F. A. H. Smith, "A Self-Analysis of Classroom Teaching," *National Association of Secondary School Principals,* **42** (March 1958), pp. 182–184.
[13] *Ibid.,* p. 183.

had gotten away from him filled this out each day and conferences were held with his principal. The device facilitated the
teacher being his own critic in that each day he was able to
analyze what went wrong, if anything, and each day he was
encouraged by any improvement that he achieved.

Another approach to teacher self-evaluation in the area of
goals and procedures is provided by rating scales. The teacher
himself has to judge what is relevant for him and what areas he
wishes to study. Suggestive ideas in a series of twelve rating
scales based on an explicit conception of the teaching and learning process are reported by Simpson.[14] The general directions
for students rating classes give the purpose, assumptions, and
specific instructions to the raters. Scale A illustrates the general
nature of the scales.

> Scale A. What is the motivational level on which learners are
>   operating?
> 1. Learner is antagonistic to procedures and resents teacher efforts
>   to work with him. Does practically no work.
> 2. Learner sees little or no value in what is done in school and
>   so only does as little as possible to keep from being embarrassed
>   or punished.
> 3. Learner recognizes goals set up by the teacher, largely rejects
>   them as valueless for him, but works because by meeting the
>   teacher's set goals he thinks he can achieve his own goals, such
>   as getting a passing mark for the course or grade.
> 4. Learner sees goals set up by teacher, accepts them as good, and
>   is working enthusiastically to achieve them.
> 5. Teacher takes major responsibility for identification and selec-
>   tion of goals and purposes but encourages learners to have
>   minor share in this process.
> 6. Teacher and learner together assume responsibility for setting
>   up sound goals and purposes and together take responsibility
>   for carrying ahead activities.
> 7. Learner assumes the major share of responsibility for setting up
>   his goals and for self-improvement; the teacher serves as a
>   guide and at appropriate times checks to see that learning is
>   continuing.
> 8. None above fits classroom. Situation described on back of rating
>   sheet.

The question at the head of each scale indicate the nature of
the content of the other scales (B through L).

[14] R. H. Simpson, "An Evaluation of Motivation, Assignment-Making,
Problem Procedures and Service Learnings in a School System," *Journal of
Educational Research,* **44** (September 1950), pp. 1–13.

Scale B. How are assignments handled?

Scale C. What practice is given in guided problem identification?

Scale D. What practice is given in guided problem selection?

Scale E. What practice is given in guided problem solution?

Scale F. What guided practice is given in trying out possible solutions to problems?

Scale G. How are evaluative abilities developed?

Scale H. What opportunities for guided practice of effective record keeping are provided the learner?

Scale I. What opportunities in learning how better to find resources needed in identifying and solving problems are provided the learner?

Scale J. What opportunities for learning abilities connected with selecting appropriate resources are given when resources are at hand?

Scale K. What opportunities are given for practice in democratic group discussion?

Scale L. What guided practice in purposeful reading to identify, select, and solve problems is being given?

TABLE 1

Normative Results for One School System

Scale	Elem.	J.H.S.	S.H.S.	All
A. Motivation	4.2	4.6	3.9	4.4
B. Assignments	2.8	4.3	2.7	3.1
C. Problem identification	3.2	4.0	3.1	3.5
D. Problem selection	3.1	4.2	3.0	3.5
E. Problem solution	3.5	4.6	3.1	3.8
F. Problem solution tryout	2.8	5.5	3.3	3.6
G. Evaluation	3.0	4.2	2.3	3.2
H. Record keeping	2.4	4.3	2.2	2.7
I. Resource finding	3.4	3.8	2.2	3.2
J. Resource selecting	3.3	4.4	2.5	3.3
K. Democratic group discussion	3.4	4.2	2.8	3.3
L. Purposeful reading	3.6	4.3	2.5	3.5
Average rating on all scales	3.2	4.4	2.8	3.4

A careful analysis of class goals and procedures can pave the way for improved discipline, better learning, and a happier teaching experience.

6

Self-evaluation in the Selection of Texts and Other Resources

Textbook selection is of major importance, since the text tends to set the organizational pattern in most American classes. Visual aids are used somewhat, teaching machines are employed to some extent, independent study is occasionally encountered; but in the vast proportion of schools in the United States the textbook sets the framework within which the teacher instructs, and presumably it provides an organizational structure which it is hoped the learner will use. Unfortunately for many learners the texts they are asked to use are so inappropriate that not only are they ineffective in helping the pupil organize his learnings but they even encourage deficit or liability learnings, such as a pronounced distaste for learning from books and an antipathy toward the subjects with which the texts are used. It should be emphasized that what is an excellently organized text from the standpoint of an expert in the field or from the standpoint of a teacher may be completely disorganized from the perspective of the student. For the latter the particular text may be totally inappropriate. Hence it is of crucial importance for the teacher to make systematic self-evaluations when it comes to the selection of texts and other resource material that he will use.

Issues for Self-evaluation in Text Selection

Three key questions may appropriately be raised by the teacher who is attempting self-evaluation in text selection:

1. Is an organized process followed in text selection?

2. Do the texts actually selected have appropriate readability levels when considered against the reading levels of prospective users?

3. Am I familiar with the characteristics of newer texts in my area?

Before decisions are made regarding what text should be used, there should be an organized selection process followed. This should first involve getting criteria that have already been developed by others or developing new criteria appropriate for the particular teachers or school. Frequently some combination of these two processes will be desirable. It is particularly important that such criteria be written down and carefully considered before their application to the actual selection of textbooks.

After a set of criteria has been either locally developed, borrowed from the developments of others, or adapted from other sets of criteria, an actual listing on a score sheet or rating form should be made for each text the teacher or the teacher committee is considering using. One actual rating form may be seen in Figure 1. It must be recognized that the appraisal process is essentially subjective; however, use of a set of rating criteria will improve the overall quality of the subjective judgments. Some may appropriately argue that this particular rating sheet puts too great a stress on certain factors to the exclusion of others of greater importance. This may be true, and each individual teacher or text selection committee should formulate criteria he or they feel to be most significant for their situation. The important thing is that specific criteria be put down on paper and then used for rating texts. Text rating is a very time-consuming process but also a very necessary one.

A second question paralleling in importance the issues considered in the preceding paragraphs is: Do the texts actually selected have appropriate readability levels when considered against the probable reading levels of prospective users? The problem the teacher typically faces in this regard is pointed up by the two distributions in Table 1. It will be noted that in the fifth grade we may expect some youngsters with average first-grade reading ability and others at the other extreme with average ninth-grade reading ability. On the ninth-grade level we

RATING SHEET
Part I

Criteria	Multiplication Factor						Remarks
Cost	X1 =						
Cover design	X1 =						
Style of type	X4 =						
Size of type	X4 =						
Layout of page	X4 =						
Pages numbered sequentially	X1 =						
Consistent placement of page numbers	X1 =						
Use of color	X2 =						
Eye appeal of pictures, graphs, and illustrations	X4 =						
Quality of paper (durable and glareproof)	X2 =						
Binding (paper or hardback)	X4 =						
Glossary	X3 =						
Table of contents	X2 =						
Index	X3 =						
Appendix	X3 =						
Appropriateness and accuracy of illustrations	X5 =						
Unit or chapter summary	X1 =						
Study, review, or discussion questions	X1 =						
Suggested activities	X1 =						
List of up-to-date resource material	X2 =						
Up-to-dateness of material	X2 =						
Reference bibliography	X2 =						
Teaching guide or manual	X2 =						
Laboratory manual or workbook	X1 =						
	TOTAL Part 1						

RATING SHEET Part II						
Main topics of course of study	Multiplication Factor					Remarks
	X1 =					
	X1 =					
	X1 =					
	X1 =					
	X1 =					
	X1 =					
	X1 =					
	X1 =					
	X1 =					
	X1 =					
	X1 =					
	X1 =					
	X1 =					
	X1 =					
	X1 =					
	X1 =					
	X1 =					
	X1 =					
	X1 =					
	X1 =					
Sequence of content	X3 =					
	TOTAL					
	TOTAL FROM PART I					
	GRAND TOTAL					
	RANK					

Figure 1. Rating sheet for textbooks. (From W. R. Miller and Robert H. Berry, "Adopting the Right Textbook," *The Clearing House*, **61** (September 1962), pp. 20–21. Reprinted by permission of *The Clearing House*.)

see that the distribution of reading abilities is likely to be even greater with the lowest reading level on the average third-grade level and the highest at a fifteenth-grade level or better. It is obvious that in any particular classroom the teacher will not find exactly any one of these distributions of reading ability;

TABLE 1

Illustrative Distributions of Reading Ages for Groups of 100 Fifth-Grade and 100 Ninth-Grade Children

Reading Grade Levels	100 Fifth-Grade Children	100 Ninth-Grade Children
15+	—	1
14	—	2
13	—	4
12	—	8
11	—	12
10	—	15
9	2	16
8	5	15
7	12	12
6	19	8
5	24	4
4	19	2
3	12	1
2	5	—
1	2	—
Total	100	100

however, distributions are likely to be similar. It should also be obvious that to select a single textbook for all of these students with all of these ranges of reading ability, even if it is appropriate on the criteria that have already been discussed, may be quite inappropriate for a majority of the students.

What are the implications of this to the teacher who is attempting to carefully self-evaluate his selection of texts? One of the most obvious ones should be that a multiple-text system must be substituted for a single-text system. This means that the teacher, instead of using a single textbook for all students regardless of ability, will use two, three, or more textbooks in order to more nearly cover the wide range of reading ability that is likely to be encountered in every class. A situation was recently called to the writer's attention in which in a tenth-grade class students ranged in reading ability from average third-grade to average sixteenth-grade plus. However, all students or their parents were required to buy a single text. It is no wonder that disciplinary problems occurred in this type of classroom, that assignments were frequently not completed, or not done at all, and that the dropout rate was fairly high. It is also interesting to note that test results on most of the students were languishing in the files of the principal's office unused by almost all of the teachers. Much time and effort had been spent by students and teachers in taking and administering and scoring the tests, but little use was being made of them. The alert teacher will attempt to anticipate what the range of individual differences in reading ability is likely to be in his classes before he settles on a particular text or preferably a group of texts for use. If in the fifth grade, for example, we were to ask all boys to wear size 4D gym shoes there would be a great hue and cry from parents and teachers, and quite appropriately so. However, as shown in Table 1, where the differences are as great in the field of reading ability, there is typically and unfortunately no hue and cry when we attempt to have all youngsters use the same textbook. It would, of course, be possible to use "supplementary material" such as tissue paper or cotton to stuff the shoes for the youngsters whose feet were too small for the average-sized shoe and to cut holes in the front of the shoes for students whose feet were too large. Obviously, this "enrichment" would not be a desirable type of situation from a physical standpoint. In a similar fashion, to attempt to make all youngsters use the same text in English, social studies, mathematics, science, or other fields is completely disregarding what has been clearly established with respect to individual differences.

What has been said implies not only that the teacher needs to know the reading levels of various individuals in his classes but that he also needs to have some methods of assessing the apparent reading difficulty levels of texts he is considering. Fortunately, there are several reading difficulty formulas available to the teacher at the present time. Most prominent of these probably are the Dolch formula, the Lorge formula, and the Dale-Chall formula.[1] Each of these permits the teacher to take a sample of pages from the text he is rating and assess the average difficulty level of the material and assign it an approximate grade level of difficulty.

A third major question for the teacher to ask himself is: Am I familiar with the characteristics of newer texts and newer resource approaches in my area? In almost every subject of study there have in recent years grown up textual differences of importance. For example, on the elementary level we have the regular text and the "classmate edition." The latter is an attempt to deal with similar concepts but in a simpler form and with less complex language. The text for slow learners and the materials for particularly accelerated learners on the elementary level have been emphasized for some time in some schools, but many teachers are not aware of the great potentialities of the spreading use of material appropriate to the student.

Many of the best teachers on both the elementary and secondary level are currently using, within the same class, several texts at a particular time. It is recommended that some diagnosis be made of each student and that appropriate texts be made available to him. For example, the new *High School English Textbooks*[2] gives a critical report based on an examination of English textbooks, including grammar-composition texts and anthologies, currently used in American high schools.

While the book is somewhat critical, especially with respect to content, editing, and organization of the anthologies, it does make some specific recommendations. For example, there are sharp criticisms of the treatment of excerpts from novels found in many anthologies. The process of specific criticism and recommendations is maintained throughout the book and should be helpful in guiding teachers and supervisors who make selective judgments about the great number of texts that they need to

---

[1] J. S. Chall, *Readability: An Appraisal of Research and Applications* (Columbus, Ohio: Ohio State University, 1958), Bureau of Educational Research Monographs, No. 34.

[2] J. J. Lynch and B. Evans, *High School English Textbooks* (Boston: Little, Brown and Co., 1964).

consider today. The emphasis of the newer texts in biology is described by Chase:[3]

The curriculum studies insist on investigatory procedures, on active inquiries leading to discoveries, on experimentation, not only to replicate or demonstrate what is known, but to step toward the unknown (at least, toward what is unknown to the student). This insistence is conspicuous and pointed in such materials as the "Block" laboratory programs and the "Invitations to Enquiry" of the biology curriculum study, but it is by no means limited to such specialized devices. On the contrary, the texts themselves are shot through and through with this emphasis. In the textbook of the physics study and in recurring chapters elsewhere, one sees the conventional textbook style of reiterated assertion of conclusions replaced by a form of discourse through which the student can perceive concepts and theory emerge and evolve from the inquiries of science.

Critical studies of texts are also available in other fields. For example, one reviewer[4] is appropriately critical of the following short paragraph entitled "Persecution of Jews" in a history text: "Tens of thousands of these unhappy people were deprived of all their property, the less fortunate were tortured to death in internment camps, the more fortunate had to leave the country and accept the charitable assistance of other lands."

The reviewer notes:

Its central statement is innocuous, inaccurate, and patronizing. The reality of the situation was that *millions* of "these unhappy people" were murdered, only a trickle were allowed to escape, and the other "lands" were not charitable in accepting the refugees.

American world history texts either fail to take notice of the Nazi mass murder or deal with it obliquely and gingerly. The following account is typical. "It reviews the doctrine of racial superiority to persecute the Jews . . . later, the storm troopers hunted down the Jews and imprisoned them in concentration camps. Many Jews fled from Germany and many non-Jews who hated the Nazi policy also left."

American textbook writers rarely make a consistent effort to provide students with deeper insight into some of the most crucial and tragic periods in recent history. It is disturbing to note how often

[3] F. S. Chase, "Some Effects of Current Curriculum Projects on Educational Policy and Practices," *The School Review,* **70** (Spring 1962), pp. 132–147. Reprinted by permission of The University of Chicago Press and F. S. Chase.

[4] M. M. Crug, "History of Textbooks in England and in the United States," *The School Review,* **61** (Winter 1963), pp. 425–440. Reprinted by permission of The University of Chicago Press.

findings of meticulous research by American and European historians
are overlooked.

When confronted with this, publishers and some authors would
probably point to the limitations of space. They might also argue that
youngsters should not be burdened with unpleasant details of man's
inhumanity to man. But that is exactly the nature of the major weakness in American history textbooks. The compulsion to "cover" the
material has often resulted in bland and ineffective teaching of
history. . . .

What is needed is to encourage more teachers to discard the
slavish "covering" of textbooks and substitute an intelligent selection
of events, issues, and problems. This would permit study in depth of
important periods of crisis in history and lead to a better understanding of the complexities of our own age. It seems imperative that more
high school students be given opportunity to study critically the concepts of democracy, fascism, communism, and the issues of freedom
and war and peace. The results might well be a much more effective
teaching of history and more effective education of future citizens in a
free democracy.

Another excellent example of analyses of 27 American history texts is provided by Palmer.[5] He concluded that only 5, or
approximately 18 per cent, contributed significantly "to an understanding of social change. . . . The great majority of these history
textbooks attempt no systematic explanation of the evaluation
of civilization." Equally challenging statements in practically
every field of study can be found and should be found by
the alert teacher seeking to improve his critical selection of
textbooks and other resources.

For the foreseeable future the basic tool for social studies
teachers, as well as for most other teachers, will be the textbook.
For this reason the ability to carefully analyze and critically
evaluate the textbook is crucial for the well-prepared teacher.
Valuable suggestions are available in a variety of fields.[6]

What are evaluative questions that the teacher can use to
get at some aspects of his work in selecting and helping learners
select resources? Some suggestive issues or self-evaluative criteria
are the following:

[5] J. Palmer, "History Textbooks and Social Change," *Social Education,*
25 (March 1961), pp. 135–136.

[6] For example, see R. Brown and M. Brown, "How to Select a Social
Studies Textbook," *Social Education,* **25** (December 1961), pp. 391–397.
Also, O. L. Davis, Jr., "Textbooks and Other Printed Material," *Review of
Educational Research,* **32** (April 1962), pp. 127–140.

1. To what degree have I developed the ability to recognize authorities?
2. To what extent am I able to ferret it out and apply in my own field methods and materials reported as being helpful in subjects other than that which I am studying and teaching?
3. Am I reviewing my use of resources sufficiently often, particularly texts?
4. To what extent has the money that my class has used for resources, including texts, been wisely used? Could much greater variety of materials, and possibly more appropriate materials, have been gotten with no more expense?
5. How effective have I been in encouraging my students to use the library and its resources?
6. To what extent do I know how and where to get needed resources which are not available locally?
7. In encouraging students to study, am I giving sufficient attention to nonprinted resources?
8. Do I encourage students to use a sufficient variety of resources including books, periodicals, interviews, actual experiences out of school, tests, questionnaires, attitude inventories, observations, conferences, and correspondence?
9. Have I thought sufficiently of helping students learn how to get appropriate resources as an important phase of their self-sufficiency in learning?
10. Have I thought of teaching students how to use appropriate resources more effectively as a significant teaching goal for me?

Sources of suggestive answers to these and many other related questions can be found in the *Education Index* under the heading of textbooks and such subheadings as bibliography, criticisms, errors, histories, illustration, publication, rating, readability, selection, and use.

After the pupil gets out of school he will no longer have the teacher at hand to locate and select all the materials he as a citizen needs. Working on the assumption that the instructor needs to gradually and progressively wean his pupils from excessive dependence on him for the locating of materials, Figure 2 suggests steps upon which he can locate the extent to which he is currently developing learner skill in finding resources.

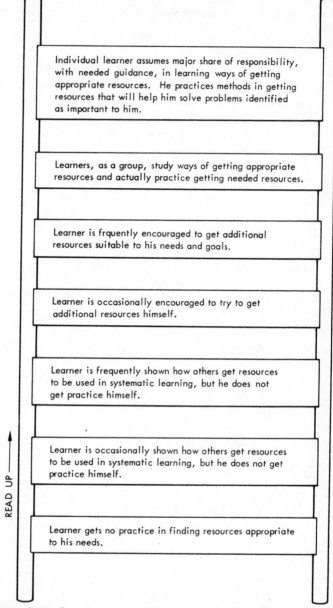

Figure 2. Finding-resources ladder. (From Ray H. Simpson, *Improving Teaching-Learning Processes* (New York: Longmans, Green & Co., 1953), p. 278. Reprinted by permission of David McKay Company, Inc.)

PROGRAMMED INSTRUCTION

Programmed instruction has been hailed by some as the major educational breakthrough of the twentieth century and has been damned by others as a misleading blind alley. Regardless of where the truth may lie between these two statements, it is incumbent on the teacher who is evaluating himself to be alert to the current issues, claims, and counterclaims relative to programmed instruction. Basically, programmed books and programs using machines are essentially the same. In fact, many programs are made available in both book and film form. For example, *English 2600*[7] is a course in elementary English grammar, which has been atomized into about 2600 "frames," each consisting of a statement with a blank to be filled in by one or two words. The student reads a frame, fills in the blank, and then turns the page to see whether he got the correct answer. There are many different forms that programming may take. A common one involves giving a sentence or paragraph or more of material and then giving one or more multiple-choice questions to which the student responds, and he immediately learns whether his response was correct or incorrect. Possibly the first self-evaluation question the teacher should raise with himself is: Am I sufficiently familiar with programmed instruction to consider and evaluate it?

Some of the relevant arguments with respect to programmed instruction are summarized in Table 2. Out of the maze of claims and counterclaims for programming and programmed instruction, what are questions to which the teacher needs to try to find answers? Following are some of the issues which the teacher needs to consider.

AVAILABILITY OF PROGRAMS?

What kinds of book programs are available in my field? What kinds of machine programs are available in my field? Which of the programs are linear and which are branched? Is good programmed instruction better than poor conventional instruction? Is good conventional instruction better than poor programmed instruction? What test data are available to show the relative effectiveness of contrasting approaches in my field?

---

[7] J. C. Blumenthal, *English 2600*, rev. ed. (New York: Harcourt, Brace & World, Inc., 1962).

Table 2

What Some Advocates Say	What Some Opponents Respond
Programmed instruction is the first major technological innovation in education since the development of printing.	Programmed instruction as now being emphasized is a blind alley.
Programmed instruction reduces teaching to an exact science and frees teachers from "ditch-digging."	Programmed instruction may be able to produce well-drilled robots, but it cannot produce creative minds.
The student goes through systematically planned questioning.	The student has no share in planning his study activities. He is like a rat in a maze or a pigeon in a cage.
Goals are carefully defined.	The learner's individual goals and developing goals are disregarded, and the machine's program assumes teacher's goals are pupil's goals.
Programmed instruction applies to humans what has been learned with lower animals.	Programmed instruction "dehumanizes" education by breaking the personal bond between teacher and student.
Principle of readiness is emphasized.	Unnecessary redundancy is rampant.
Teachers will not have to dispense information or correct homework.	There is no substitute for personalized interaction between teacher and student.
Mistakes on meaningful auto-instructional material are harmful.	Students learn from their mistakes and most gains can be made on difficult items.
Programmed instruction provides variety.	Programmed instruction over a period of time is likely to become deadly boring.
Programmed instruction is economical in freeing the teacher for more productive work.	Programmed instruction is enormously expensive at $50 to $500 per student original outlay, with expensive repair service; also, new booth and room arrangements will be a large added expense.

Table 2—Continued

What Some Advocates Say	What Some Opponents Respond
Automatic, programmed instruction teaches facts as effectively as conventional procedures.	Current research has been short term and spotty. The effects of long-term programmed instruction are unknown.
The program decreases cheating and laziness.	The program in book form may actually encourage cheating and laziness.
One *active* response after another makes sense.	Research shows reading the material without active response is just as effective and more economical.
Human learning is basically the same as animal learning.	Most human learning differs in important respects from animal or rote learning.
Programmed instruction is an educational bonanza.	Programmed instruction "is responsible for some educational monstrosities."

Does the Crowder approach, "branching," or the Skinner approach, "linear," probably hold more promise for me in my teaching? In investigating programmed instruction should I consider using machines linked with such resources as film projectors for visual demonstrations, or linked with tape, television, and phonographic playbacks, or linked with a variety of other library materials?

TEACHER COMPETENCE AND ATTITUDE?

May some combination of programmed instruction and conventional instruction be best for me in my stage of professional development? If so, what combination might it be, and how can I best go about determining this? What would I as a teacher need to know and be able to do to use programmed instruction effectively? How important is teacher attitude toward programmed instruction in determining its effectiveness? Some research makes it appear that this aspect is crucial.

STUDENT ABILITIES AND ATTITUDES?

In my field is programmed instruction likely to be better for those of high intelligence or those of low intelligence? Which kind of instruction is likely to be best for the well motivated? Best for the poorly motivated? Are the trial and feedback most important for learners who have to be kept at the task with artificial controls or for those who are strongly self-motivated to keep at learning tasks? Research in the area of foreign language instruction suggests that teaching a foreign language to elementary-school children in its cultural setting is a potent force in creating more positive attitudes toward the peoples represented by the language. The research also suggests that newer educational media, such as television, through especially designed programs may be more effective than personal contact with classroom teachers in establishing particular attitudes.[8]

RESEARCH ON PROGRAMMED INSTRUCTION

To what extent is what is found to be true in one teaching area true in my field in general and for me in particular? How can I determine this? What kinds of interpretations and appropriate responses can be most economically taught through programmed instruction? Is programmed instruction most effective with highly structured material where there are definite correct answers and least effective in developing creativity and divergent thinking? Will the generalized, verbal concepts learned through programmed instruction transfer for use in concrete, nonverbal situations? Should autoinstructional material be an adjunct to, rather than in place of, established educational materials?

The teacher whose self-evaluation reveals some deficiencies relative to programmed instruction should find it interesting to look up some reviews and interpretations of research in the field. For example, the articles by Sidney L. Pressey, "Programming—Boom or Bust?"[9] and by Harry F. Silverman, "Self-Teaching Devices and Program Materials,"[10] are of great value in getting some initial orientation. Both of these give references that could be useful to the teacher who wishes to follow up suggestions and get additional ideas relative to the field.

The kinds of questions raised in the preceding section are

---

[8] M. A. Riestra and C. E. Johnson, "Changes in Attitudes of Elementary-School Pupils Toward Foreign-Speaking Peoples Resulting from the Study of a Foreign Language," *Journal of Experimental Education,* 33 (Fall 1964), pp. 65–72.

[9] *Teachers College Record,* 65 (February 1964), pp. 413–418.

[10] *Review of Educational Research,* 32 (April 1962), pp. 179–193.

illustrative of issues that the teacher can appropriately deal with in such fields as television teaching and instruction by language laboratories. For example, a recent monograph by Keating[11] raises serious doubts about the effectiveness of language laboratories. His report discusses in detail a study of 5,000 students of French in 21 school systems of the Metropolitan School Study Council. His findings: In two areas of language instruction, students, who did not use language laboratories scored consistently higher than those who did; there was only one instance where the language laboratory was superior. When Keating's findings were recently made public, they gave rise to widespread expressions of concern. The alert teacher in the language field certainly should examine research such as this in order to know what the evidence is relative to newer trends. The teacher in other fields, such as English, social studies, mathematics, has a similar responsibility for studying the research available concerning the effectiveness of newer approaches in his area of major concern.

An illustration in English is described by Bruell.[12] He analyzes the problems involved in fitting paperback books into an already crowded program without dispensing with any of the essentials. It was decided that all reading should be done outside of class. It was also decided that many composition assignments should spring from explorations in the paperback work. Problems of emphasis were also considered important. For example, should concentration be in the narrative, which is most popular, or in exposition, which is most utilitarian, or on sturdy argumentation. How could students become so interested in books that they would want to take them home and keep them and use them? These and other issues can be appropriately explored by the self-evaluating teacher.

In conclusion it appears that self-evaluation is likely to lead the teacher toward (1) more systematic and analytical selection of texts, (2) more use of multiple-text approaches to help take care of individual differences, and (3) more familiarity with and facility in the use of a variety of nonconventional text materials such as filmstrips, movies, records, television video tape, and programmed materials.

[11] R. F. Keating, A Study of the Effectiveness of Language Laboratories (New York: Institute of Administrative Research, 1963).

[12] E. Bruell, "The Paperback Comes to Bremen High," The English Journal, 51 (January 1962), pp. 33–38.

7

Self-evaluation and Personality

As has been suggested in the preceding chapters, adequate teacher knowledge of subject matter and of appropriate goals, procedures, and resources is of great importance. Also of paramount importance is the teacher's understanding of himself. It has been suggested by Myers[1] that "understanding of the self is the most crucial of all understandings." If the teacher is accurately to interpret the behaviors of others, he should have a comprehensive picture of himself.

Does teacher personality make a difference? After eight years of research in nine public schools, Washburne and Heil[2] indicate:

> The one striking result of the experiment has been clear evidence that the teacher's personality has a clear and measurable effect on the progress of her pupils academically and socially—academically in terms of progress on the *Stanford Achievement Test,* socially in terms of friendliness and recipiency of friendliness as measured by the *Ohio Social Acceptance Scale.* There appears to be a relationship between the type of teacher and her children's emotional adjustment as shown on the children's feeling tests.

After a comprehensive study involving several thousand people in one way or another, Jersild[3] concluded:

[1] K. E. Myers, "Becoming: For Child and Teacher an Ever Changing Self-Image," *Childhood Education,* 41 (September 1964), pp. 35–38.
[2] C. Washburne and L. M. Heil, "What Characteristics of Teachers Affect Children's Growth?" *The School Review,* 68 (Winter 1960), p. 425. Reprinted by permission of The University of Chicago Press and C. Washburne.
[3] A. T. Jersild, *When Teachers Face Themselves* (New York: Bureau of Publications, Teachers College, Columbia University, 1955), pp. 13–14. The excerpts that follow are reprinted by permission.

It has become increasingly clear over the years, as the work in this inquiry proceeded, that self-understanding requires something quite different from the methods, study plans, and skills of a "know-how" sort that are usually emphasized in education. . . . a teacher cannot make much headway in understanding or in helping others to understand themselves unless he is endeavoring to understand himself. If he is not engaged in this endeavor, he will continue to see those whom he teaches through the bias and distortions of his own unrecognized needs, fears, desires, anxieties, hostile impulses, and so on.

The process of gaining knowledge of self and the struggle for self-fulfillment and self-acceptance is not something an instructor *teaches* others. It is not something he does *to* or *for* them. It is something in which he himself must be involved.

The importance of self-evaluation and self-improvement in the area of teacher personality is paralleled by the size of the difficulties involved. However, Burt,[4] for example, concluded that self-rating is second only to life-record methods for accuracy in personality measurement. When used with cooperative individuals, self-rating ties for first place in accuracy.

Two interacting types of perception are closely related to teacher personality: self-perception and perceptions related to pupils. In an attempt to help the teacher evaluate himself, various facets of these types of perception will next be discussed.

SELF-EVALUATION OF SELF-PERCEPTIONS

As has already been noted, the understanding of self is possibly the most crucial of all understandings. Combs[5] has pointed out, "Perceptual psychology indicates that the behavior of the individual at any moment is a function of how he sees the situation and himself. . . . The behavior of a teacher like that of everyone else is a function of his concepts of self." Success in this area can be improved by examining and re-examining certain important issues the teacher may appropriately raise with himself:

1. Do I perceive my success as being closely tied up with the success of others? More specifically do I see my professional

[4] C. L. Burt, "The Assessment of Personality," *British Journal of Educational Psychology*, 15 (1947), pp. 107–121.

[5] A. W. Combs, "The Personal Approach to Good Teaching," *Educational Leadership*, 21 (March 1964), pp. 369–377, 399.

success as being largely determined by the success of the pupils with whom I work? In art, authorship, or research the lone wolf may be very successful. However, it is very difficult to see how a teacher's success can be divorced from that of his students. The teacher who is smug and self-satisfied with "his high standards" when over 25 per cent of his students fail would not seem to meet the criterion suggested here.

2. Do I visualize myself as a crystallized, completed person or as an intellectually and behaviorally learning person? The former type of individual is likely to be so "mature" that his ideas are outdated and his intellectual outlook is backward. The active, professionally growing person, regardless of chronological age, not only will be critically examining new events but will also be an active learner who is challenged by the quantity and diversity of what he does not know, such as the infinite complexities of young people and their relationships with their peers and with adults. The teacher who perceives himself as one who has completed his learning and who sees his job as one of "dishing it out" is bound to slip backward. One cannot stand still. He who is not learning professionally is going to be deteriorating professionally.

Carl Rogers[6] suggests that the continuous becoming of an individual must include his willingness to be a process that is ever changing. This becoming continues throughout the life-span. Some mistakes will be perceived as an inevitable part of the learning process. The learning person is one who can take a disappointing situation and learn something useful from it.

3. Do I cultivate a flexible self-assurance in myself? After an extensive study of teachers with contrasting success records, Olander and Klagle[7] listed emotional maturity first among the four best predictive measures of success. It has been shown that teachers with an "integrative" pattern of conduct show significantly more spontaneity, initiative, voluntary social contributions, acts of problem solving, and fewer negative attributes such as

---

[6] "What It Means to Become a Person," in C. E. Moustakes (ed.), *The Self* (New York: Harper, 1956).

[7] H. T. Olander and H. M. Klagle, "Differences in Personal and Professional Characteristics of a Selected Group of Elementary Teachers with Contrasting Success Records," *Educational Administration and Supervision,* **45** (July 1959), pp. 191–195.

conflict with others and boredom.[8] The need for developing flexible self-assurance is very understandable, since the typical working day for teachers is more than nine hours, and more than half of this time the teacher is responsible for leading a dynamic working situation in a group of 20 to 40 active young people.[9] Myers[10] has described flexible self-assurance in the following fashion:

The replacement of fears and anxieties by self-assurance which can accept good times and bad and yet remain intact gives one knowledge that the self-image can shift if the occasion demands and incorporate the shift into the changing perception of what it means to become. Teachers who have this flexible self-assurance which allows them to change to meet the new and ever changing classroom challenges, can help children achieve self-assurance.

4. Do I perceive myself as a person who not only tolerates diversity of point of view and procedure but even welcomes it? Am I comfortable when two students disagree on a subject appropriate for class discussion or, even more crucial, when a student takes issue with me? Lack of appropriate perception toward diversity may be shown by irritation when controversial issues are discussed. Lack of tolerance for diversity of opinion may also be reflected in a desire to quickly give "the answer" in a discussion rather than encourage the clash of differing perspectives and the probable accompanying sharpening of intellectual abilities.

With desirable perspective the teacher will encourage an atmosphere where each student will not be afraid of being labeled foolish if he proposes a creative or offbeat idea even if it is extreme.

The teacher with a favorable perspective toward himself and diversity will avoid such expressions as: "The only way to teach _____ is _____." "The only good text in my field is _____." "The only way to solve the crisis in southeast Asia

[8] C. C. Anderson and S. M. Hunka, "Teacher Evaluation, Some Problems and a Proposal," *Harvard Educational Review,* 33 (Winter 1963), p. 73.

[9] NEA Research Bulletin, "Teacher Time Devoted to School Duties," *Education Digest,* 28 (February 1963), pp. 43–45.

[10] "Becoming: For Child and Teacher an Ever-Changing Self-Image," by Kent E. Myers. From *Childhood Education,* September 1964, Vol. 41, No. 1. Reprinted by permission of the Association for Childhood Education International, 3615 Wisconsin Avenue, N.W., Washington, D.C.

is _____." The traditions of democracy and the healthy search for the truth are not promoted by dogmatic assertions which reveal an intolerance for stimulating speculation and an honest search for the truth.

Not only in educational issues but also in such fields as politics, economics, and art a realistically tempered intellectual vitality is hard to maintain without the constant challenge of divergent ideas.

5. Do I see myself as a person able to discuss my own personal and emotional problems? Do I accept and even seek criticism as a part of my personal and professional development?

As the teacher looks inward upon himself he inevitably sees areas of doubt and uncertainty in his search for meanings and values. The comprehensive study by Jersild to which reference has already been made suggests that excessive personal tension may appear "in disproportionate resentment, competitiveness, discouragement, efforts to impress or placate, to play the game and play it safe."[11] The study further showed that most teachers when given the opportunity found discussion of their anxieties and doubts a very useful venture. Jersild's interpretation is this:[12]

> Facing the issue of anxiety meant, to them, a way of sharing a human situation with intimate personal meaning. The discussion of anxiety was a discussion of something that to them was *real,* even if painful. It was something that involved them personally, instead of telling them, as so many discussions in education do, how to do something to somebody else. It penetrated to some degree the wall of isolation that keeps people emotionally separate from one another.

SELF-EVALUATION AND TEACHER PERCEPTIONS OF PUPILS

The preceding section has emphasized that the teacher's self-perception is strongly influential in determining his behavior. The teacher's needs, attitudes, tensions, and anxieties not only strongly condition his self-perceptions but also influence his perceptions of his pupils. Clarification and better understanding on the part of the teacher of his assumptions and perspectives

---

[11] Jersild, *op. cit.,* p. 9.
[12] *Ibid.,* p. 64.

with respect to his pupils are likely to decrease undesirable biases and distortions which would have adverse effects upon the teacher's leadership of learners. In this section we are concerned with issues that the teacher may appropriately raise with himself in better understanding his perceptions of his pupils.[13]

1. Am I sensitive to the private worlds of my students, particularly as these relate to me? In my interactions with them do I accept their perceptions, feelings, attitudes, beliefs, and understandings as extremely important? These issues are particularly significant to the teacher when a pupil's perceptions are at variance with his. Myers[14] suggests, "Teachers must be open to complete self-evaluation, for they must see themselves through children's eyes to evaluate the 'self' the children see. Children's evaluation is often an eye-opener for teachers who perceive themselves only through their own senses. . . . The critical examination of self is a difficult task, as self acceptance must be achieved."

The teacher should be aware that his complex perception of pupils and the related ongoing interaction of him with them will be conditioned by a number or processes wich have been revealed by careful experimentation in social psychology. According to Secord and Bachman[15] these include (a) "the tendency to see persons as unchanging entities," (b) "the tendency to see the cause of a person's actions as lying in him rather than in the situation," (c) "the coloring of perceptions by favorable or unfavorable evaluations of the stimulus person," and (d) "the placing of persons in ready-made categories associated with sets of personal attributes." Knowing that these things happen can alert the teacher as to prospective difficulties in relations with pupils, such as the danger of stereotyping as indicated by (d) above.

2. Am I primarily *person oriented* rather than thing or event oriented? A teacher's training all too frequently is almost exclusively tied in with things (that is, in history, mathematics).

[13] For a number of these issues the author is indebted to Arthur W. Combs, "The Personal Approach to Good Teaching," *Educational Leadership*, 21 (March 1964), pp. 369–377, 399.

[14] *Op. cit.*, p. 3.

[15] P. Secord and C. Bachman, *Social Psychology* (New York: McGraw-Hill Book Co., 1964), p. 90.

The current emphasis on things and events is usually accompanied by a relatively small number of contacts with pupils of the age with which the teacher will later be working. Thus, it is very easy for the prospective teacher and the teacher to get into the habit of giving excessive weight to things and events and insufficient weight to pupils and their perceptions.

Not only is the good teacher person oriented but he likes persons. Keliher[16] states it this way: "He is interested in them (children), is intrigued by their way of doing things, likes to watch them grow in mind and body, enjoys their emerging accomplishments. This teacher knows about the rough edges of growth—that boys and girls need help and guidance—that this is the reason for teachers."

In Ryans' six-year study,[17] which involved 100 separate research projects and over 6,000 teachers, he concluded that three of the key characteristics that differentiated between good and not so good teachers were: (a) the good teachers had attitudes favorable to pupils; (b) they enjoyed pupil relationships; and (c) they were generous in their appraisal of the behavior and motives of other persons.

3. Am I *meanings and significance* oriented rather than exclusively facts oriented? This question implies the need to learn more about the interpretations and meanings that pupils do or should attach to some of the factual learnings. It suggests a need for the teacher to learn more about the perceptual experiences of his students, about why their perceptions may lead them to reject an assignment, about why the youngsters may believe that most of what they find in their texts is "phony." The growing teacher is concerned with how things seem to the pupils, for their ideas may turn out to be radically different from the teacher's. This difference, if unperceived by the instructor, may seriously interfere with learning.

4. In my contacts with a pupil do I characteristically look for causes of his difficulties on which I can possibly help him rather than shrugging off his behavior with statements such as:

---

[16] A. V. Keliher, "Environment for Learning," *Education Digest,* 28 (February 1963), pp. 12–15.

[17] D. G. Ryans, "Some Relationships Between Pupil Behavior and Certain Teacher Characteristics," *Journal of Educational Psychology,* 52 (1961), pp. 82–91.

"Look at his mixed-up family, what can you expect?" or "His parents are divorced, he has no father, his mother works, you can't hope for much," or "He doesn't even know when to come in out of the rain"?

Much more constructive questions which give promise of eventual improvement in the pupil are ones like these: Why is the text I am using possibly inappropriate for this pupil? Which reading material would probably be better for him? How might I modify the nature of my assignments, possibly by giving optional ones so that the pupil will perceive the study to be of potential value to him? I have perceived the pupil as "failing." In what respects am I as the classroom leader "failing"?

It is always easy to find a variety of alibis for our failures, but it is much more challenging, and much more effective, to search for constructive changes we can make in our own behaviors so that the pupil is more likely to succeed. The great potential in the wealth of professional reading materials should not be neglected when behavior changes are considered.

5. Do I regard each pupil as being capable? The traditional concept that each pupil in a particular class should be able to do "the work" of that class is an unfortunate legacy. It is a social vestige that prevents many teachers from dealing effectively with with individual differences in varied goals, assignments, use of resources, and class procedures. When we really accept individual differences, we will recognize that the below average pupil can do as well *in terms of his abilities* as the above average student if we are capable of helping create a learning situation where each is expected to do according to *his* abilities.

Secord and Bachman[18] have concluded that "persons exhibit a general tendency to assume that others are similar to themselves." If a teacher denigrates his pupils or colleagues, there is a rather strong suggestion that he is unsure of his own abilities.

6. Does the personality I have developed encourage a love for learning? Possibly the greatest weakness in our schools today resides in our current inability to do an effective job in instilling a love of learning in our pupils. This suggests that each teacher has the responsibility to study each aspect of his approaches to teaching and attempt to determine which of his

[18] *Op. cit.*, p. 91.

behaviors probably are promoting a longtime interest in teaching and which, even though they are getting immediate results, are probably killing the desire to learn after the teacher is no longer around.

Two incidents reported by Hughes[19] illustrate contrary approaches: "A third grade child read to his class about dinosaurs, pronouncing the words, 'tyrannosaurus' and 'brontasaurus' without hesitation." After this feat the only response the teacher gave was, "You left out an 'and.' " This would possibly be expected to have a negative effect.

Contrast that incident with the second one: "One morning Charles clomped into Sister Teresa's second-grade, leaving a trail of large daubs of mud. He brought a bird with a broken wing held tenderly in his hand. After the bird's wing was attended to and the bird placed safely in the cage, Sister Teresa said, 'Charles I know you are worried about the bird today but tomorrow you will take the mud off your shoes before you come into the classroom.' " The situational and perspective understanding illustrated here can contribute much to the fostering of a love for learning more about the great unknown.

TEACHER BEHAVIOR REFLECTS PERSONALITY

Since a teacher's personality is reflected in his behavior one method in examining his personality is to determine what his behavior reflects. That such behavior also affects children's behavior is illustrated in a study by Kounin and Gump[20] in which they selected three pairs of punitive versus nonpunitive first-grade teachers in three elementary schools. Each of the 174 children in these six teachers' classrooms was interviewed individually about what he thought was "the worst thing to do in school." He was also asked why he thought these misconducts were bad. The researchers concluded that, as compared with

[19] "Teacher Behavior and Concept of Self," by Marie M. Hughes. From *Childhood Education*, September 1964, Vol. 41, No. 1. Reprinted by permission of the Association for Childhood Education International, 3615 Wisconsin Avenue, N.W., Washington, D.C.

[20] J. S. Kounin and P. V. Gump, "The Comparative Influence of Punitive and Nonpunitive Teachers upon Children's Concepts," *Journal of Educational Psychology*, 52 (February 1961), pp. 44–49.

children who have nonpunitive teachers, children who have punitive teachers "manifest more aggression in their misconducts, are more unsettled and conflicted about misconduct in school, are less concerned with learning and school-unique values, show some, but not consistent indications of a reduction in rationality pertaining to school misconduct."

Some indication of the relationships between pupil and teacher classroom behavior may be drawn from studies by Ryans.[21] He found that

. . . for elementary school classes, *high* positive relationships were noted between observers' assessments of "productive pupil behavior" (e.g., assessments presumed to reflect pupil alertness, participation, confidence, responsibility, and self-control, initiating behavior, etc.) and observers' assessments of previously identified patterns of teacher behavior which seem to refer to understanding, friendly classroom behavior; organized, businesslike classroom behavior; and stimulating, original classroom behavior.

For secondary school classes, *low* positive relationships appeared to obtain between productive pupil behavior and the above-named categories of teacher behavior, with a tendency for the stimulating, original teacher-classroom behavior pattern to show a slightly higher correlation with pupil behavior than the understanding, friendly or the organized, businesslike teacher behavior patterns.

It should be emphasized that while relationships have been established in such researches as Ryans' there is not yet proof of direct causal or producer-product relationships.

An additional type of semantic analysis is provided by Ryans in his teacher characteristics study.[22] One of twenty-five dimensions of teacher behavior which he analyzed was the "harsh-kindly" dimension, and the following descriptions are provided by Ryans:[23]

Harsh	*Kindly*
1. Hypercritical, faultfinding	1. Went out of way to be pleasant and/or to help pupils; friendly
2. Cross; curt	2. Gave pupil a deserved compliment
3. Depreciated pupil's efforts; was sarcastic	3. Found good things in pupils to call attention to

[21] Ryans, *op. cit.*

[22] D. G. Ryans, *Characteristics of Teachers* (Washington, D.C.: American Council on Education, 1960).

[23] *Ibid.,* p. 88.

Harsh	*Kindly*
4. Scolded a great deal	4. Seemed to show sincere concern for a pupil's personal problem
5. Lost temper	5. Showed affection without being demonstrative
6. Used threats	6. Disengaged self from a pupil without bluntness
7. Permitted pupils to laugh at mistakes of others	

Although Ryans' listings and descriptions were made primarily for other purposes, they can be quite helpful to the individual teacher in self-evaluation of aspects of behavior that may significantly affect teacher-pupil relations.

Since Ryans' teacher characteristics study is the most impressive study of this type, the notable differences between the teachers rated high and those rated low are of significance. These have been summarized as follows:[24]

> There was a general tendency for high teachers to: be extremely generous in appraisals of the behavior and motives of other persons; possess strong interest in reading and literary affairs; be interested in music, painting, and the arts in general; participate in social groups; enjoy pupil relationships; prefer nondirective (permissive) classroom procedures; manifest superior verbal intelligence; and be superior with respect to emotional adjustment. On the other hand, low teachers tended generally to: be restrictive and critical in their appraisals of other persons; prefer activities which did not involve close personal contacts; express less favorable opinions of pupils; manifest less high verbal intelligence; show less satisfactory emotional adjustment; and represent older age groups.

Evaluative Questions the Teacher May Use to Check on Teacher-Pupil Relationships

The teacher can appropriately construct his own questionnaire which will give him some feedback relative to his relationships with pupils and a reflection of his own personality as perceived by pupils. Typically it is desirable to have such feedback of an anonymous nature. Illustrative questions[25] the teacher may use are shown in the following:

[24] *Ibid.*, pp. 397–398.

[25] Adapted from R. H. Simpson and J. M. Seidman, *Student Evaluation of Teaching and Learning* (Washington, D.C.: American Association of Colleges for Teacher Education, 1962).

Open-Ended Illustrations

1. How do you find the relations between teacher and pupils in this course as compared with other courses you are now taking?
2. What is the general "climate" of the classroom (e.g., relaxed, tense, warm, cold, friendly, hostile, etc.)?
3. Why is your relationship with the teacher in this class better or worse than with other instructors?

Checklist Illustrations (Check those which apply.)

4. Students:
   ____enter freely into activities
   ____appear relaxed
   ____are orderly without specific directions from the teacher
   ____are noisy, disturbing
   ____work concentratedly
   ____are restless
   ____participate halfheartedly
   ____are rude to teacher and/or each other.

5. ____Students feel free to discuss various aspects of the course with the teacher.

6. ____Teacher seldom available for conference with student.

7. ____Students feel free to discuss personal problems with teacher.

8. ____Teacher provides students with many opportunities to make decisions.

9. What is the feeling between the instructor and the students?
   ____excellent mutual understanding and good will
   ____better human relations than in most classes
   ____about average
   ____not as good rapport as in most classes
   ____little mutual understanding, poor human relations

10. Instructor's attitude toward students:
    ____always courteous and considerate
    ____usually courteous and considerate
    ____unsympathetic and inconsiderate
    ____arouses antagonism of students

11. Instructor's fairness:
    ____absolutely fair and impartial to all
    ____usually fair
    ____has some favorites in class
    ____constantly shows partiality

12. If I have a problem relating to the course, my instructor:
    ____seems definitely annoyed when I wish to discuss it with him
    ____discusses it with me, but acts as though I am bothering him
    ____seems willing to discuss it with me
    ____generally acts as though he wants me to discuss it with him
    ____definitely encourages my discussing such problems with him

13. Class decisions—the teacher:

____meets difficult situations with poise and confidence

____occasionally loses poise

____frequently loses control

14. Class atmosphere:

____too formal and uncomfortable

____formal but not strained

____warm, democratic; class and instructor work together

15. Student-instructor planning:

____instructor encourages student participation in planning and organizing class objectives and activities

____instructor allows students' suggestions and criticisms to influence his plans for class objectives and activities

____planning is chiefly by instructor; instructor is indifferent to students' criticisms and suggestions

____planning is by instructor, and student participation is discouraged

16. The group methods used have been:

____very valuable

____somewhat valuable

____of little value

____of no value

A systematic study of pupil responses to questions such as the preceding illustrations can form the basis for improvement which should later be reflected in improved pupil perspective of the teacher and in more desirable learnings.

8

Self-evaluation and Interpersonal Relations with Colleagues

THE MODERN TEACHER is not strictly an autonomous individual whose domain is his own classroom. One dimension in evaluating the quality of the teacher in the modern school is reflected in his attitude toward and his working relations with colleagues. The suggestions in the following paragraphs are designed to be provocative, to suggest ways that the teacher may wish to evaluate his current relationships with his colleagues.

Am I professionally mature enough in an emotional sense to welcome and use criticisms from colleagues? Because of past background or training, or more probably lack of appropriate training, many teachers today are geared consciously or unconsciously to resent suggestions and ideas coming from others which might be used in self-analysis. Consequently, one of the first questions the teacher needs to raise with himself concerns his emotional maturity in the area of criticisms from others. Rather than regarding criticisms as attacks on our personality we should think of such analytical comments from others as potentially quite valuable in helping us to improve our own professional activities. A doctor should not resent it if a colleague suggests that there may be something wrong with him physically that needs to be modified or changed. In a somewhat similar fashion we as professional workers in education should not object to, but rather should welcome, helpful analytic comments that may come from colleagues.

One indication of the significance of interpersonal relations

for teachers is indicated in a study of values by Rosenberg.[1] His
data show that 57 per cent of "people-oriented" individuals re-
mained teachers in a two-year period (1950–1952) while only 19
per cent of "nonpeople-oriented" individuals did so. This seems
to indicate a greater early dropout among the nonpeople-
oriented. It is also quite possible that of those who remain, considerable dissatisfaction is caused by immature interpersonal
relations.

*Have I informally assessed my colleagues to determine which
ones can give the most professional help of various kinds?* For
example, do I know which fellow workers can probably refer
me to printed sources of professional ideas of particular sorts
which I might use? Do I know which colleagues are likely to
have stimulating ideas on specific issues, such as ways of grouping students? Do I know which colleagues are likely to be able
to help me most if I have disciplinary problems of a certain
type? Do I know which colleagues are apparently most successful in arousing in students a significant interest in learning and
more learning?

*As part of my regular work week, do I systematically try to
get helpful ideas from colleagues?* This may be done in the lunch-
room, at a break between classes, over coffee, before school, after
school, at teachers' meeting, at any time when contact is made
with other colleagues. Much of this can be done quite informally, but it is surprising how many useful ideas a teacher can
pick up over a period of time if he systematically raises questions
with fellow workers. For example, the teacher may ask the colleague, "Have you read or would you be interested in reading
the latest issue of *The School Review?* I would be glad to let
you borrow my copy, since I would be interested in your reactions, particularly to the article starting on page 86." Or again,
the teacher may take a recent professional book to a colleague
and ask him if he would be willing to give his reactions to parts
of it, to a certain chapter, or to the general purpose of the book.
The teacher may have just returned from a particular conference
or workshop or convention and has picked up some literature or
some ideas about which he wishes to have reactions from col-

---

[1] M. Rosenberg, "Factors Influencing Change in Occupational Choice,"
in P. Layerfeld and M. Rosenberg (eds.), *The Language of Social Research* (New York: The Free Press of Glencoe, 1955), pp. 250–259.

leagues. This provides good grist or an entree for a useful discussion at that time or later on when both have more basis for mutual discussion of the material under consideration. Such reciprocal help not only is potentially very useful to the teacher initiating the verbal interchanges but can prove valuable to other colleagues. Such activities also tend to build up professional morale in a school system.

One particular type of colleague who can be of considerable help and who is frequently available if the teacher is interested is the supervisor. Of course, the supervisor's primary job is to get others to work more effectively, more productively, and to stimulate reflection and professional growth. If the teacher looks at him in this light, then the teacher can approach him, describe some of his difficulties or some of his apparent weaknesses, and get constructive ideas and help.

On invitation from the teacher, the supervisor may accept the role of classroom observer with the number of visits depending largely on the teacher's and supervisor's purposes. Typically, each such visit should be followed by a conference, at which time strong points in the teaching-learning situation are emphasized and possible ideas for improvement are discussed. Sometimes mutual use by the teacher and the supervisor of an evaluative instrument is desirable.[2]

In most situations the supervisor can be effective only if the teacher willingly goes for aid to the supervisor and tries to get help. In this way, the relationship between the supervisor and the teacher can be a favorable one. For a successful relationship to be built, the teacher must be in a receptive mood. Consequently, the primary responsibility must lie with the teacher and his systematic searching for ideas for improvement, which lays the foundation for help to pass from the supervisor to the teacher. The supervisor is likely to be able to work effectively only if the teacher tells him what he is trying to do, ways he has tried to go about it, and requests ideas from the supervisor as to what additional approaches might be more effective.

[2] For examples and ideas see L. S. Vander Werf, *How to Evaluate Teachers and Teaching* (New York: Rinehart and Co., 1958), pp. 30–31. Also, R. H. Simpson and J. Seidman, *Student Evaluation of Teaching and Learning* (Washington, D.C.: American Association of Colleges for Teacher Education, 1962).

Am I sufficiently tolerant of the approaches and ideas of other teachers? Not only must the individual teacher attempt to solicit ideas from others, but he must also consider the possibility that what others are doing may actually be very desirable and very useful, although quite different from what he is accustomed to or what he currently believes to be desirable. Almost all new materials and most of the old ones are still not conclusively demonstrated to be effective. The same is true for most teaching methods and teaching procedures. Consequently, it behooves the individual teacher to be extremely tolerant of the ideas, goals, materials, and procedures of colleagues. Not only may we not be able to demonstrate that they are undesirable, but it is necessary for desirable morale and for a favorable atmosphere for students to learn that teachers work together as a unit regardless of the fact that they have different ideas and different approaches. The developing teacher is one who recognizes there may be much good in the work of colleagues and is very slow to make critical comments to others about a particular colleague. Where the teacher feels impelled to comment or criticize he should typically raise questions with the teacher involved rather than with students or with other colleagues.

What responsibility does the teacher have for considering and attempting to improve the organizational structure under which he works? Many teachers operate as if the organizational structure within which they work were handed down from on high and could not be changed. Actually, one of the best contributions that some teachers can make is to evaluate the relationship of the current organization to themselves as teachers and then to work to improve and change the setup. For example, some administrators[3] believe that the ordinary organization of a school predisposes people, especially those on the teaching level, to feel alienated. They feel that attempts should be made to change the business-military style, with a hierarchy resulting in the board and superintendent at the top and teachers and children in an inferior position. They feel more suggestions from teachers could be useful. If a teacher feels that some aspect of the administrative setup could be improved, most administrators are happy to have suggestions. Requests for materials and re-

[3] R. L. Foster, "A Climate for Self-Improvement," *Educational Leadership,* **21** (February 1964), pp. 275–276, 321.

sources typically get a good reception from the administrator.

Some of the joint problems that teachers, supervisors, and administrators face are suggested by the following conversations, which take place on a Thursday afternoon.[4]

In the school superintendent's office—*Assistant Superintendent:* "Principal Jones doubts whether he can get the teachers in his building to go along with the new schedule."
Superintendent: "Too bad. We put a lot of thought into the reorganization. The principals did too."
Assistant Superintendent: "Why are teachers so resistant? Reasonable requests meet with apathy and grumbling. They're so short-sighted they harm their own best interests."

In a corridor—*A Supervisor:* "I wish we could get teachers to take more responsibility. Another teacher from Mr. Jones' building sent back the projector without the cord."
Another Supervisor: "I don't blame teachers. The administration ought to provide a pickup service."
First Supervisor: "Maybe so, but all the directions are written out. The trouble is they won't read them."

In a coffee shop—*First Teacher:* "I'm exhausted. We had visitors from the office. Then there was a meeting about a joint English-history program. Imagine trying to correlate English with the history Mr. X teaches!"
Second Teacher: "That's what the new consultant brought to town. These things come and go. You work out something for somebody to publish a book about and then it's over."
Third Teacher: "It's too bad, for the children suffer. We do too. The pressure gets worse every year."

Nylen and Bradford[5] diagnose this situation as one lacking appropriate intercommunication, with personnel insulated against understanding the feelings, purposes, and problems of others. No proposal will work in every situation but the educator may give consideration to such ideas as the following:

1. Take up problems with current, local teacher organizations.
2. Try to get the perspective of those with whom we take issue.

[4] D. Nylen and L. P. Bradford, "We Can Work Together," *NEA Journal,* **37** (October 1948), pp. 436–438. Reprinted by permission.
[5] *Ibid.*

3. Study articles and books giving research on improving human relations, such as *The Planning of Change*.[6]
4. Suggest one or more problems for planned consideration in faculty meetings.
5. Suggest possible use of human relations experts in the school.
6. Study books on group dynamics such as that by Cartwright and Zander.[7]
7. Develop skills useful in meeting human relations problems in the classroom and in colleague relationships.

Do I set an example to the students I teach by effectively working with other teachers? In their classrooms, many teachers emphasize the need for cooperation on the part of the pupils, then turn around and disregard their own dictum when it comes to working cooperatively with other staff members. Example is likely to be stronger than precept, and if the teacher really believes in the need for cooperative activity, he himself will set an example by cooperatively working with colleagues in his school.

Such work may take many forms. It may, for example, involve curriculum construction or curriculum changes that tend to be an important part of cooperative teacher work at the present time. It may involve evaluation of some aspect of the work of the school, some aspect of reading, listening, writing, mathematics program, the science program, or some other program the school is cooperatively attempting to implement. It may involve modifying the current reporting system.

Typically such evaluation is likely to be somewhat slow and laborious, particularly if teachers have not had much experience in it. However, as teachers gain experience, as they become more willing to give and take constructive criticism concerning what they and others have done, there will result a general upgrading of the professional activities in the school.

The cooperative effort with other teachers may in some cases involve team teaching, which typically causes a redefinition of the formal relationships among staff members. It may create

---

[6] W. G. Bennis, K. D. Benne, and R. Chin (eds.), *The Planning of Change* (New York: Holt, Rinehart and Winston, 1961).
[7] P. Cartwright and A. Zander, *Group Dynamics, Research and Theory* (Evanston, Ill.: Row, Peterson and Co., 1960).

9. What are the contributions of nongraded or ungraded schools through which each child progresses at his own best rate without regard to annual promotion from grade to grade?

10. Should new school buildings be constructed with movable soundproof walls that will make it possible to teach large groups sometimes and smaller groups at other times?

11. Is the psychology of the teacher as important as the psychology of the learner for improving teaching-learning situations?

12. How can we better assess the transfer value of what is being taught in our schools to make them of greater value and service to members of our community?

13. Are the scheduling problems and inconvenience to teachers caused by television worth the effort? What are the effective uses of television?

14. What kinds of in-service training programs is it most desirable for us to work on?

15. How can our big city schools desegregate when housing is still segregated?

16. How can the most talented, the brightest, the most creative, and the most imaginative students be attracted to teacher education?

Have I used any diagnostic tools to help better understand my characteristics and my interpersonal relations? Personality characteristics can sometimes be better understood if one or more tools are self-administered and the results studied. A comprehensive listing of potentially valuable tools can be found in *Tests in Print*.[10] Critical reviews of specific character and personality tests can be found in *The Fifth Mental Measurement Yearbook*,[11] as well as in earlier yearbooks edited by O. K. Buros.

An example of a recently developed diagnostic instrument of interest to teachers and administrators is the *Occupational Characteristics Index*.[12] This is a brief self-administered tool based on

[10] O. K. Buros, *Tests in Print* (Highland Park, N.J.: The Gryphon Press, 1961).

[11] O. K. Buros (ed.), *The Fifth Mental Measurement Yearbook* (Highland Park, N.J.: The Gryphon Press, 1959).

[12] Developed by R. H. Simpson, M. Slater, and R. Stake, University of Illinois, Urbana, Illinois.

combinations of twenty-one characteristics which various researches have suggested are related to effectiveness in teaching.
Self-administration of a tool of this sort can help the teacher
identify those characteristics in which he is strongest and those
in which he probably needs to improve if his success in working
with others is to be improved.

DATE DUE

DEC 26 '71			
Faculty 74/5			
GAYLORD			